CHIGGERS IN MY TEA

An Expat's Survival Guide

Being a Collection of
Poems and Themes and Advice
by

Bernie Bruen

1ˢᵗ Edition

Copyright © Bernie Bruen 1996

TABLE OF CONTENTS

Schnappfulwerkenkaike -- Last Night's Pasta
Sauce -- Mazaudet Fridge Cull Tart -- **Mother Bruen's
Very Best Tomato Sandwiches** -- Sugarless Marmalade
-- East of Suez Fish Curry -- Formula One Curry --
Tomato Soupe -- A Warming Pig Stew -- Simple Pig
Casserole -- Soupe de Biere -- Wild Pumpkin -- Easy
Pasta -- **Finest Buttered Egg** -- **Mrs Bruen's
Celebrated Fudge Pudding** -- Nottalott Stew

THE LAST RESORT
In Search of the Maori -- A Sailor's Dream of Devon --
End pieces

DEDICATION

For

Robin Swaine, Alistair Halliday

Richard Farrington, David Ince

and

all the 'Gavvie Boys'

-oOo-

not forgetting

my 'oppo', Rob Hoole,

Ernie and Elizabeth Page

of Edinburgh

and

Greg Powlesland

ABOUT THE AUTHOR

Son of Second World War Naval Fighter Ace -
Commander J M *'Bill'* Bruen DSO DSC RN, Nigel
Bruen, or just *'Bernie'* as he is better known, was brought
up in the tradition of the Royal Navy and in appreciation of
all things nautical, natural and musical. This was enhanced
by his education at The Old Malthouse Prep-School and
later at Wellington College.
Having failed to enter the Royal Navy as a pilot at 17 years
old [*"I wouldn't trust this boy with a bicycle – let alone a helicopter."* G
Stainforth – Master of Wellington College], he turned his attention to
the Theatre, attending the renowned Pam Chapman's
Birmingham School of Dramatic Art, and working in
various Repertory Theatres, before becoming Stage
Manager of the famed John English's Midlands Arts
Centre at the early age of nineteen. He soon branched out
into experimental Light Shows, producing both
Hytesenemic and Psychedelic lighting, with his own
Company - 'LX84', working in the process with many of
the top Pop Groups of the late Sixties.

When the Navy once again issued its magic call, he
entered Dartmouth Royal Naval College, at age 22, as a
trainee helicopter Pilot but subsequently, finding that
flying was not his 'thing', transferred to Seaman
Specialisation. It was at this time that he qualified as a
Diving Officer (while still a Cadet) and joined that
specialisation that would prove so effective in his ensuing
career.
There followed the usual round of Junior Officer
appointments, mostly at sea, during which time his love of

that environment and the Ships in which he served became apparent through his writings, songs and poetry. Ever the practical man however, he began to make a reputation for himself as a Mountaineer and as a Seaman, attributes inherited directly from his Father.
By the mid Seventies he was established as the above and also, although a late starter, was becoming well known in the sport of Boxing.

1976 was the year when his life started to move in a definite direction, however, as it was then that he qualified as a Mine Clearance Diving Officer. By this time he was also part of the RN Boxing Squad (the only Officer to have achieved such a distinction without having risen through the ranks) and was becoming well known as a Performer of Sketches and Songs, as one half of Folk Duo *'Rattlin Down'*.
He ended his boxing, at the age of 33, as Scotland RN Champion at light-middleweight and runner-up to the European Silver Medallist in the Navy Open boxing competition; also, bizarrely, as British Indian Ocean Territories light-welterweight champion.

There followed five busy years:
as First Lieutenant of the enormously successful *'HMS Gavinton'*;
as Executive Officer of an obscure Naval Party in the Indian Ocean (which is what happens if you upset somebody);
and as the Captain of a Fast Patrol Boat in the Straits of Hormuz, on loan to the Oman Navy just as the Iran/Iraq war started in 1980.

He returned from those disputed waters in time to be sent to the Falkland Islands for the Conflict there; as officer commanding *'Fleet Clearance Diving Team Three'*, whose achievement of 66% awards for *'Brave Conduct'* was unequalled by any other involved Unit (he, himself, was awarded the Distinguished Service Cross for removing live 1,000lb bombs from *'RFAs Sir Galahad and Lancelot'*). He became the first man since Korea to defuse an unknown, enemy sea-mine by hand; despite not being allowed the proper equipment to do so.

After a term as Bomb Disposal Officer to Flag Officer Plymouth, he was again appointed to *'HMS Gavinton'* - as (it later transpired) the Last Captain; having by now been selected for promotion to Lieutenant Commander. During the next two and a half years the Ship achieved considerable success, particularly during the Gulf of Suez Mine Clearance in 1984, for which action he was made MBE; they being the first ever to locate a live, unknown enemy mine by high definition sonar.

Following his ship-command, he returned to the Falkland Islands for a time, in charge of the Clearance Diving Team there. On return to UK, he set up and commanded the first team of high-specialist Maritime Counter-terrorist Divers (qualifying as an operational parachutist at the age of 40!), remaining with them until he took voluntary retirement in 1988.

He went back to the Royal Navy of Oman in a Training roll at that time and then served for five years as Executive

Officer and Sailing Master in the Sail Training Tall-ship '*SNV Shabab Oman*'.

Promoted to Commander's rank, by the personal wish of HM the Sultan, he then retired from the sea, married the 'Splendid Patricia' and they now live in deepest, rural France, where they have made a comprehensive 'wild-life garden'.

INTRODUCTION

The volume **'Ratlin-Down and Redding-Up'*** was
originally produced as an unofficial appendix to that most
excellent tome **'Flowers of the Sea'** by Eric Bush, which
any Sailor would be well advised to have in his Ditty Box.
This Book, **'Chiggers in my Tea'**, is in itself an addendum
to the first and, in consequence therefore, a further
appendix to the second. It contains previously unpublished
pieces, in the main un-connected with the Sea, that have
been written over the last twenty five years and was
mustered during 'watch-below' time, at sea in a Tall Ship.

> *My luck is a Flower*
> *Scattered into a Thorn-bush*
> *And gathered barefoot*
> *On a very windy day*
>
> *The Flowers of the Sea*
> *May be gathered in the Wind*
> *For there are no Thorns*
> *Hidden in the passing waves*

-o0o-

Onboard ship, off-watch and relaxing, sailors were
encouraged to let their hair down at certain times - the
'pipe' being made:

"Hands to Dance and Skylark!"

At such times they would gather together, on the upper
deck if the weather was fine or in the mess-deck if

inclement, and entertain each other with music, song and story, which would often be interspersed with more serious readings and recitations, as the mood took.
On one occasion, some fifteen years ago, when some such folk were busily engaged in practising the said situation, with frenetic jigs and reels, a fellow Officer was heard to remark,

"Play us a sad tune - to make us happy."

It is this feeling of counter-point that enhances the buoyancy of light heartedness by giving pause for thought and reflection. Visit any Variety Show and you will see how this juxtaposition has become a tried and tested formula that keeps the entertainment alive; alternately lifting spirits to increasing heights and gently letting them quieten before a further crescendo is reached.

So it is that this volume is presented - to amuse, enlighten and, perhaps, provoke thought.

'Chiggers in my Tea' is in reality the landsman's version of the sailor's *'Rattlin Down'*. It is written for the Expatriate, a man as much 'at sea' with regard to the norm as is the sailor. Each will find as much to interest him in the one book as he will in the other.

Of course there are no 'Chiggers' at sea and it would be a rare occasion indeed to experience the process of 'Rattlin-down' ashore; but that makes it all the more fun - and isn't that what this whole business is about?

Bernie Bruen
Wudam (on the mud)
Sultanate of Oman
1996

*Later published as 'Songs and Ditties of the Fleet' ISBN
978-1-84683-143-0

FROM FAR AWAY TO HOME

The 'Gentleman Adventurer', who sailed the Seven Seas in Ancient Times, had as his highway the Middle Sea (Mediterranean), the Red Sea, the Black Sea, the Baltic Sea, the North Sea, the Arctic Sea and, if he was brave enough to venture there, the Ocean Sea (Atlantic). Now, in the Modern Era, there are more available Seas *'than you can shake a wicked stick at'* and adventuring has become widespread, safer and probably a good deal easier.
Do not be misled, though, for it seems as though the process may be reversing. Global Warming, the Greenhouse Effect, natural and man-made disasters are all combining to *'upset the apple cart'*, as it were, and turn the whole thing into the proverbial *'bag of worms'*.
Winds of amazing ferocity have begun to make their appearance around the world and the established weather patterns are being disrupted. Things are changing and travel may be about to start getting *'...a bit dodgy, folks'*.

Going away from home has changed considerably in the last fifty - no - thirty years. Just hop on a 'plane' and you will be whisked half the world away in a matter of hours; that is providing that you do not mind paying a fortune to be squashed like sheep into back-torturing seats, lacking in leg room, head room and elbow room - particularly elbow room.
OK, so the food is not that bad and the booze is free (or used to be), but there is not much of the first and the second is not needed except as an anaesthetic. But who can eat anyway, when at the mercy of the fidgety man on one side, a hugely overweight passenger overflowing the

adjoining seat on the other and the precocious child kicking at the footrest behind? It is impossible to drink coffee in the bounce of turbulence (the only time it is served) and the incessant crying of the infant alongside its sleeping parents, somewhere in the vicinity, precludes that precise activity.

Happily the flight will soon be over and how often do you do it anyway?
Once a year on holiday?
Perhaps.

But there are others to whom it is not that simple. They are the people who work abroad; people to whom 'Home' is but a visiting place.

The Americans live in America. The Romans live in Rome. The Italians live in Italia, but the Englishman lives 'at Home'.

The 'Expat' (expatriate) is an ancient export from UK and is to be found wherever one may travel in the world. He is, in himself, a strange creature - part adventurer, part mercenary and part failure. Seen seldom in his native country, his conversation there will contain references and tall-tales (but quite true ones) quite beyond the appreciation of his neighbours; who will often remark aside that *'he spins a good yarn'*, but will not readily believe the truth of it.

They are the ones, these rooted bystanders, who have their houses in order; whose lives are regulated by their own willingness to succumb to the commonplace. They look upon the Traveller as a somewhat quaint individual, perhaps to be indulged as an eccentric until he should once again *'go foreign'*.

He is the oddball, the peculiarity; the man who *'.....has not got it quite right but will probably settle down in the end.'*

Certainly our Wanderer is different and, with any kind of imagination, will wrest the most from his experiences abroad; also he may just be better off financially than his more staid acquaintances; for that is most likely his reason for working so far away from his homeland in the first place.

But no matter how good life seems, no matter how much money he makes, the fact remains that his place of work is not *'Home'*, nor can it ever measure up to that exacting standard. Recessions, devaluations, crises, changes of Government, even wars may wrack the land of his birth; it will not matter. Home is *'Home'* and maintains that in-definitive magnetism that makes it fonder to the heart by the very absence that tugs at the latter's strings.

So, as the 'resident' Englishman returns home to a cosy fire, (tea nicely laid out by a devoted wife, slippers warmly ready for tired feet, his book on the table *(where he left it!)*, children dutifully waiting to greet 'paterfamilias' and the family pet drowsing on the hearth), perhaps he will spare a thought for the Expat sitting in his cement-clad, breeze-block house, the air-conditioning 'wall-banger' whining incessantly, as he watches yet another badly-recorded video or muses on his chimerical lot.

QUOTIDIAN

Can I compare this sharp and dusty Palm
To veined leaves of Chestnut, Beech or Oak?
Can I relate the sterile, wind-blown sand
To fallowed earth that's tilled by Devon folk?
How can the Donkey's bray,
Heard from the date tree brake,
Measure against the warmth
Of the Pigeon's cooing wake?
The stark of concrete holds no sentiment
That thatched roofs of Tudor barns evoke.

Can heated, shattered rock be lyricised,
As slow hills of Dartmoor's green are cloaked?
Are humid, stifling winds of Araby
Remindful of the winter fire that smoked?
Where are the rustling leaves?
Who hears the Dog Fox bark?
How would the Turtle lay?
How fare the cruising Shark?
There can be no abutment, no rapport;
Only sad dreams,that restless nights provoked.

['*Quotidian*' was the winning entry in the Oman Literary
Competition (foreign contributions) in the mid 1990s]

The images that beset the mind in the dark hours of sleeplessness are, by turn, the Expatriate's bane and his salvation; and generally it is only possible to interpret their significance by the stirring emotions briefly felt as they vanish in that very moment of waking.

Soon enough even those impressions die and all that remains is a forlorn feeling of either sad- or happi-ness to haunt the newly wakened hour. The mind grapples to recapture the lost thought and, in that struggle, so does the evasive doorway of sleep softly close its portal tight and fast. The gift of slumber is denied. The limbo of the awful night stretches ahead for hour upon hour, depicted by a half seen but thoroughly understood glimpse of the watch face's luminous message.

As he lies on his iron truckle-bed, sweating beneath the shroud-like winding of a sodden sheet; as Chit-chats* stalk the ceiling above and cockroaches scurry across the concrete floor below, the occasionally adventurous one climbing-up to tangle in his hair; as the fan whirrs overhead with that maddening squeak that no amount of oiling will eliminate; as he rolls his head from side to side, comforted and mind-dulled by that incessant movement; he will think of those familiar things that make England – *'Home'*.

THE LANE

High hedge bent by six hundred snows
Hawthorn berries brightly shining
Half-grown oak in hiding

The smell of a fox
Holly darkly biding
Honeysuckle softly twining
High swallows in telegraphed rows

(*Chit-chat: a small house-lizard, adept at clinging to smooth walls and ceilings, whose darting movements help to rid the dwelling of insects. It gets its name from the occasional sound it makes, which is far preferable to the incessant, thought-piercing chirping of the cricket.)

In the daily round of life abroad, one concept resurfaces time after time - the Traveller is a guest in someone else's land. He may be surrounded by other 'exile' friends; he may be so attuned to the area and culture that he thinks to have made himself a second home; but this is not so.

It is illusion.

Familiarity does not a native make nor, despite the best intentions, the finest relationships and the closest feelings of co-operation, does it engender ultimate acceptance.

In the final recourse he is on his own out there.

In such situations it helps to have a creed. Many turn to religion, others turn to drink. Probably the largest group finds solace in endless rounds of Golf; itself a quasi-religious affair much akin to Freemasonry.

Yet perhaps our Wanderer would serve himself better to leave behind these convenient social placebos and find a bridge between his present circumstances and that treasured place his inner yearning seeks; for it is there and, with a little effort, a little self-reliance and a belief in his own mysteries, it can be his.

PRESERVATION

Sink slowly into green and windswept hills,
Whose purple rocks are buttresses of truth.
Defy the cunning, soul-ensnaring ills
And leave them chase their vigil after youth.
Let passions fly, nor yet your will enfold

But join the creatures of the moors and streams.
Think their thoughts; their freedom always hold;
Make this belief the lynch-pin of your dreams.
Protect it in the mantle of your heart
And walk where only others' thoughts can be.
Allow your capture - so to 'come its part
And thus, in such communion, set you free.

There is no peace in the city, except perhaps in
Central Park - yet that is overlaid with the vibrant roar of
traffic, laden with fumes, and beset by thieves and robbers
in their hour.

To walk along *Regent's Street, Acacia Avenue or The
Shambles* - is to pass between the ghosts of trees from
centuries before. Among those wraiths are the shades of
phantom animals peeping coyly from behind the spectral
boles; but yet they are invisible to the common eye.

They are alien to the care-worn City dweller, his life beset
by mediocrity and driven onwards by an overwhelming
desire to attain its own, lowly standard.

He cannot see the wolf, with the tongue-lolling grin, loping
down the steps of *Lloyds Bank* to traverse the pelican-
crossing in total disregard of the *'wait'* light. Nor can he
delight in the fierce tussle of the forest boars as they vie
for the favours of the over-anxious sow. The otter and her
cubs play alongside the family of foxes over by the storm-
drain and badgers forage through the supermarket check-
out; but he sees them not.

How can he? He is late for an appointment and the busses
are full. Everyone seems to be going the other way as he
battles wearily on towards his goal, mentally rehearsing
excuses.

But the Traveller has time to think in his far-away land;
and anyway it is evening there and work finished six or
more hours ago.

He can see what they cannot and has the time to
remember.

FOREST

Walking naked through the forest
Two dragonflies in tandem flight
Perched upon the outstretched
Fingers of my hand
The squirrel's skelter fetched
Him up with standing wonder bright
And in his liquid eyes expressed

Sometimes it is best just to let the fancy wander freely into the ether and then to see what ideas it brings back upon its return. This is impossible in the city. There is too much smother to allow such delicate transport; unlike the air of foreign fields where the spirit can soar, travelling to far-off, unseen places - to reappear with magic in its train.

THE BIRCH GROVE

The mightiest mass of rock and strength
That reaches upwards to the sky
Meets the softness of the clouds
To stand unmoved in place and time.
Below, the damp and silent folk
Will pause and listen to the Voice
That they have known throughout their lives;
A music of undreamed-of peace
That floats and eddies through themselves;
Utopia elysian,
A haven of forgotten thoughts,
A golden awning over marble towers
That shimmers, whispers in the air,
Self to self,
Group to group
All to all
And each to each.
So many, like a nation, cluster on the slope,
Their thousands still and full of peace.
As yet untarnished by the outside world,
These sculptured pillars stand in majesty,
Candles in the night of day

With golden coins a-twinkling in their flames;
A beacon guide to home and peace.
They are the creatures of the childhood of the Earth.
The Sculptor of the Wilderness created them
And Heaven mirrors in its courts of hope and love
The restless peace that glimmers here,
To cheer each lonely visitor
Who waits to enter Paradise above.

There is a place in Arabia, far away from fog and snow, as yet un-visited by tarmac roads; a rugged double-fissure in a rock-bound coast, that even the citizens of that distant land know little of.

Its existence is 'fish' and has always been so. It has not changed much in the twenty five years that the country has taken to transit from the 13th to the 20th century - beyond the replacement of wooden dug-out *'Hoories'* by fibre-glass sea-boats, polystyrene floats on the fishing nets and, of course, *'Mr Yamaha's Wonderful Up-wind Sail'* - the ubiquitous outboard motor.

Now the place is made noisy with its roar as the long white boats indulge in the first of their only two speeds - fast or stopped. Their curving wash laps at the oyster-encrusted shoreline, where the rocks are under-cut by a million nibbling tides, and dissipates its waves among the scrubby tree-bushes that stand in the salt water of the lagoon.

But in the tranquil hours, from 1pm to 4pm, when all the Arab world is asleep, the Time-machine takes the land back to its beginnings.
Then comes out the Englishman alone (no, there are no Dogs about) to witness its fulfilment.

AT BANDAR KAIRAN

What fish flew? What men were wed?
What sights have these shores seen?
Were I a gnarled and ancient tree,
Perhaps these things I could reveal.
Perhaps you see them now or feel
Their ghosts, where ghosts have been.

Leaves but grow. Roots burrow deep.
The branch shall twist and strain
And stand forever in the sea
Where Allah chose they should fulfil
His water-picture; and they will,
At his command, remain.

Old am I; skin creased and lined;
The jebbel-sea spawned man;
My lineage beyond your time.
Your wealth will quickly pass you by.
My wealth, the land, the sea, the sky,
Remains at Bandar Kairan.

(Jebbel: Arabic word for mountain.)

Sometimes it palls - the sunny clime, the easy life. Ennui,
that soft, unwelcome visitor, creeps slowly in and besets

the most spirited mind. Monotony and tedium
engender apathy, bringing with it a world-weariness that
eats away at the *'will to do'*.
For there is a sameness about the arid lands, dramatic
though they might be with grandeur, that can never surpass
the Homeland's wet and windy setting.

Then the Expat longs to return; longs to shake off the dust
of travel and to plant his roots firmly and deeply in the
moist soil of his native land - never to stray again. The
colours are the key. They are an abiding reminder of where
he is and of where he wants to be.
Beneath it all there niggles in his brain the need to change.
He wants only to crawl back into that warm familiarity that
links his earliest memories with a burgeoning dislike of his
self-inflicted banishment. The feeling grows within,
despite his best endeavours, until it owns him mind and
soul.
It strangles at his heart. It whispers in his ears. It tugs
insistently at his T-shirt sleeve.

It is not enough to plunge into the cooled and cooling
swimming pool, nor to order yet another *'Chapmans'**
from the steward as he stretches out on his sun-bed lounger
amid the bougainvillaea and the sculptured palms.
The trips inland up ragged waddis to picnic in a far oasis
have lost their charm.
The water-ski and parascend have relinquished their lure.
Not only a change of pace is in order, but a different
lifestyle highly recommended.

Perhaps it is time to go to Sea again.

LEAVING

Oh how I long to leave this monochrome landscape,
brown on brown, blasted by the vitreous sun.

Oh how I long to see the colours of England,
green on green, gentled by the windriven rain.

Oh how I long to see her rivers once again
and, in leaving, leave these sands of time to run.

Chapmans: No one seems to know just who Chapman
was but, whoever he was, he left behind a legacy of great
value.
In hot countries alcohol is the great enemy, yet it is
pleasant to indulge in the physical act of drinking and fluid
intake is essential. Nothing, it seems, can equal the
particular pleasure given by a cold pint of beer [remember
'Ice Cold in Alex' ?]
Chapman came pretty close, however, with his concoction:

A Pint glass
A Dash of Lime juice
Angostura Bitters
Lemonade and/or Tonic to fill up
Ice

(The advantage, of course, is that large quantities of the
stuff can be drunk without becoming so.)

And so the Voyager puts out to sea again in his sailing
boat - - perhaps in a Drascombe Long-boat. The wind

blows, always it seems from the direction in which he wishes to travel and yet his ship sails on.

> *And it's Westward-ho! For Chideok,*
> *For Titchbourne and Carhaise,*
> *And come-about a hundred times a day.*
> *Sailing from Suwaddi, the sunset all a-blaze*
> *With a head-wind dead against you all the way!*

(Chideok, Titchbourne and Carhaise – names of three Drascombe long-boats, sailing out of Wudam-on-the-Mud, towards the Suwaddi Islands – half a day away)

The white canvas swells a pregnant curve that answers to his longing and soothes it to tranquillity. The mind is eased and the breeze blows the yearning away.

Maybe he will take his course far up to the north of the *Arabian Peninsula*, where lies the Strait of Hormuz. Its southern periphery is the rocky promontory of '*the Mussendam*', set in the sea like an errant part of the Norwegian coastline.

In the days of round-the-world cruising in the Great Liners, when things to **see** far surpassed mere 'shopping', there were certain sights that were an absolute must for the traveller. There was *'The Rock'* (of Gibraltar), *'The Canal'* (Suez) and, in Oman, *'The Bend'*. Cruise-liners would

steam up Oman's north east coast and approach
Mussandam Island.

Passing between this and the mainland, in a gap barely
200metres wide, they steamed through '*Fac al Assad'*, or
'*the Lion's Mouth'*; for the rock formations on either side
looked exactly like crouching lions – of the type one sees
in Trafalgar Square.

The ship would then move on to '*Perforated Rock'*, now no
more - it fell into the sea in the late eighties - and round to
the small town of *Khasab.* Here lies the entrance to *Khor
A'Shams (the Fiord of the Sun)*, the hottest place at sea on
earth. The highest temperatures ever to have been recorded
by a ship at sea were taken here.

Entering into this khor, with precipitous cliffs rising sheer
on either hand, the sun beating mercilessly between them
to make the heat monstrous, the Liner would make a ninety
degree left turn to follow the sinuous waterway.

This was the infamous *'Bend'* and here lay the football-
field-sized *Elphinstone Island*, whereon were stationed
employees of the Cable and Wireless Telegraph relay-
station that connected India with Egypt (and all points
north and west) by undersea cable.

This tiny island, with whitewashed buildings perched upon
it, was about as remote an outstation as it was possible to
find anywhere in the world. There was no air-conditioning
for them in those days; there was little water and rations
were only supplied infrequently, apart from those
supplemented by local trade; and it was hot, damned hot.

It was no wonder that, with little else to do beyond the
work of the station, those who were there became

deranged or, as the saying came to be, went *'round the bend'*; for that is where they were - round the *Bend of Khor a'Shams*. Then they were carted off to recuperate at the Indian mental asylum at Dhoolali, up in the foothills. This was known as *'going Dhoolali-tap'*.

Both these sayings: *'going round the bend'* and *'going dhoolali'* have since entered the English language and firmly remain there.

KHOR A'SHAMS

The Sun that sets on Khor a'Shams,
If He has done his work a-right,
Will burn the <u>core</u> from living man
And leave him <u>shamb</u>ling in the night.

It is a peculiarity of returning to England from the Middle East that, on the first morning back Home, the leave-taker will wake at 3am; his time-awareness still being regulated by the muezzin's call from far-off minarets.

Nothing could be finer than to walk the deserted country lanes at this time for, like at Bandar Kairan in the mid-day sleeping, the Time-machine is at work here too.

SECRET WORLD

Soft grey to deep black,
Outlines of trees
Stretching far into oblivion.
What wondrous things
Are enfolded in your dark
Secret world?

The own hoots
Its soft, far-reaching cry
Of plaintive loneliness,
And the wind blows
From a thousand miles.

The sky,
Like an echo chamber,
Sends me all the hidden sounds
In a sightless world.

Again the owl hoots,
The sound searching for an ear
To marvel and wonder
At such a call.

And so the silent trees
Look down in amusement
At man's unending failure.
The grass talks to the poppies
Who lift their heads
In simple magnificence.

What unseen life goes by
Undiscovered
When all the world sleeps?

Leave over, the respite enjoyed; recuperated, renewed, invigorated; the Expat is glad to be back in his adoptive country where the pace of life is easier and the sun always shines. He sees it anew through eyes from which the cataracts of 'ennui' have been couched and is able once more to appreciate in full the special flavour of the place.

Like his first, early morning foray back at Home on leave, our Rover will take his first sortie, perhaps to the local Market, there to renew old acquaintances with the Traders and Artisans, all of who know him and who welcome him back with a handshake here and a cup of coffee there. He stops for a while to watch .....

THE LEATHER-WORKER

Leaping tuna stitch a silver
Pattern through an oily swell.
Weaving sailfish draw their lazy,
Rippled lines in parallel.
Smaller fry, to best escape, leap
Headlong for a watery sun
But, from the very air, the patient
Tern will snatch them one by one.

Sitting, stitching silver thread, the
Leather-worker's fingers flash,
Weaving golden strands in lazy

Lines, with thoughts from calabash.
Sudden splashes, whorls and spirals
Please the mind, arrest the eye
And here and there a bead, a jewel
Bid's you welcome; bargain; buy.

Muscat, in the Sultanate of Oman, not too far distant from *Bandar Kairan* (see earlier), is a harbour that shouts the word 'impressive'. It is surrounded by Peaks, or so it seems. The appearance is that of a closely regimented array of mountain-tops dumped along the coast to form a forbidding, yet safe haven for ships and mariners*. **Horatio Lord Nelson** himself visited here when a young Lieutenant and left his mark in the painting of a White Ensign and his Ship's name, *'HMS Persus'*, on the rock of *Khor Muscat*. Since then scores of ships have done likewise and the outer island of the haven is adorned with a 'history' of visiting ships going back a couple of hundred years. Now-a-days it is preserved as a National Heritage Site.

The *Corniche* that runs along the shore is very twentieth century, yet just above it stand the old Portuguese forts and even older Omani watch-towers that date back hundreds of years.

MUSCAT WATCH-TOWERS

Crumbling crags protect this barren shore;
Lonely watch-towers, perched on lofty spires,
View with gaze that saw conquistador.
Ghosts of weathered warriors survey,
Cunning in the ways of jebbel war.
Listen in a bold creative flair.
Hear the swords unsheathed, the musket's roar;
See their sunken, staring, sand-rimmed eyes,

That, wary, watch these borders evermore.

* non-sequitur:

'*Mariners*' are surface-seafarers. '*Submariners*' are those who man 'under-sea-boats'.

Do not call them '**Sub**-*mariners*', as that would imply that, as far as seafarers are concerned, they occupy a lower stratum – as in '*humans*' and '**sub**-*humans*'. Better by far, and more polite, to call them '*Submarine-**ers***', for that is what they are – people who venture forth in submarines. It doesn't matter what they might like to call themselves (for maybe they have not properly thought it through); do not stoop to that discourtesy - by suggesting that they may not be all they wish they were (all evidence notwithstanding).   Anyway, as far as I am aware, no Submarine has ever entered Khor Muscat.

FRIVOLITY

An absolute essential for the Traveller is a sense of frivolity. He should equip himself with a selection of songs, recitations, stories and verse in the lightest vein to amuse and entertain those with whom he meets upon the appropriate occasion.
A 'party piece' is as fundamental to his outfit of kit as his Ditty Box or second set of spare socks.

The Summer Ball given by the Governor of The Grand Bahamas would be the ideal opportunity to display a virtuoso talent for playing a musical instrument, for example. Should he not be gifted in this particular field however, a fine singing voice capable of rendering a comic song successfully would prove equally acceptable to the Wayfarer and the Company.

The ability to 'speak after dinner', particularly one given by the Resident Commissioner of the British Indian Ocean Territories, could make the difference between the guest room with the air-conditioner and the spare bedroom with the ceiling fan.
Songs around the campfire in the High Veldt or the Outback will be doubly welcomed, particularly if unfamiliar to fellow campers; and a corrugated-iron Bar in the swamps of New Guinea could easily be enlivened with Riddle and Rhyme.

The section that follows contains an assortment of such pieces, along with notes on their presentation and performance.

The Voyager should take care to practice them beforehand in order to get the right nuance for his personal style. If possible he should learn them by heart so that he is not encumbered by having to hold the book in his hand in order to read the words; however, if that is the way it has to be, then the performance should be conducted as a 'Reading' rather than an 'Act'.

Each will be successful provided that it is rehearsed sufficiently to prevent any interruptions to the 'flow'.

THE VICTORIAN MUGGER

Start with a clear call, as if from a distance, but in a cultured voice that is *'....bright with fellowship'*.
As the lines progress, imagine that you are approaching your victim.
Reduce the volume and modulate the voice to that of a *Sea Captain* and then a *Policeman* (as indicated in brackets).
Finally, in the last two lines, use the confidential yet threatening tones of the East London Thug, as caricatured so brilliantly over the years by **Arthur Mullard** in so many British Lion films.

(bright fellowship)
"Stop!
Hold hard.
Be still.
Attend.
Your journey now delay.

(sea-captain)
Desist your motion.
Curb your speed.
Let fly.
Heave-to.
Belay.

(policeman)
No more advance.
Remain.
Arrest.
Reduce your speeding wash;

(Arthur Mullard)
And kindly pass your wallet
Or I'll hit you with this cosh."

-oOo-

It is always useful for the Wanderer to have a couple of tongue-twisters in his repertoire. Everyone knows from childhood the universal:

"Peter Piper picked a peck of pickled pepper.
Here's the peck of pickled pepper Peter Piper picked."

Equally famous are:

"Round the ragged rock the ragged rascal ran."
and:
"How much wood could a Wood-chuck chuck if a Wood-chuck could chuck wood;
but a Wood-chuck can't chuck wood so a Wood-chuck couldn't chuck wood, could 'Chuck?"

Here are two that are a little different; perhaps not so hard, but fun none the less.
(Interestingly, they were written, along with others in this book, to slow down the speech of young **Ordinary Seaman Albert Kirk RN**, in **'HMS Blake'**, years ago. He used to speak so rapidly that nobody could understand a word that he was saying; and he was in danger of being unable to pass, what were then, the very stringent tests required before becoming an Able Seaman. He did pass and has since gone-on to become a highly respected Warrant Officer in that Branch.)

THE KNACK

The knack of getting

A slack yak into
A track-shack is
A smack on the back.
Or,
For the lack of a whack,
To avoid any flack,
Pack the hack in a sack,
Jack it and stack it in
A rack with a snack
Under a black mac.
Whack up a kack-plaque
With a tack and you've cracked it!

The second tongue-twister, or perhaps more of a
'aspirantial-acrostic' , is this one below. It slows down the
delivery to allow one to breathe – for breathe we must.

HERMAN

*"Herman, the huge Hungarian, has held hundreds of
ostriches hostage.
Having hitherto helped heave heavy helves homewards, he
has hacked half a hundred hafts from a haggard huddle of
half-hearted handcuffed Halberdiers. Hamstrung by a
handful of hairy hamsters, he happened to harpoon a
handsome, heartless, harlotry harridan holding a hateful,
haunted hassock, who hoisted hoards of honeymooning
hobgoblins and horsewhipped her humanity into
haphazard houseboats."*

-o0o-

DRAGONFLY

This is a nonsense-song which, if it is sung absolutely
'straight', should engender sympathetic and good
humoured groans from the audience at the end of each
verse. The tune is that which introduced the world to the
long running and, in its day, successful US situation
comedy - *'The Beverley Hillbillies'*, starring, among

others, that fabulous character actor and ex-dancer –
Buddy Ebsen.

I once had a brother who was a dragonfly,
Who dragon-flew his dragon-flight across the dragon-sky.
He'd chase the female dragons 'till off his dragon-head
Then he'd 'trap' their dragon sisters and drag 'em into bed.

This dragonfly wrote poetry in his special way.
He recited it to everyone he met each dragon-day
And every time he finished, they each said, every one,
"I'm sure it's very good but it does drag on and on."

He saw a hairy dragon and he thought he knew the face.
He'd seen it somewhere, sometime in some far-off dragon-
place.
But when he heard it shout, "Hurrah! Come on lets sack
the toon!"*
(He said,) "It's not a dragon - but a hairy Scots Dragoon."

Then came the Christmas Pantomime and dragons
everywheres
Flocked into the Dragon Hall and flew around the chairs.
My brother, with his special act, was very quickly fetched
When someone shouted, "Dragon! Get your 'drag' on.
You're on next."

Chorus:
Dragons in the belfry and dragons in the bar,
Dragons in the drawing-room and dragons in the car,

Dragons who were arsonists and couldn't get it
right,
Breathing fire and brimstone 'till they set themselves
alight.

* A Glasgow accent could be advantageously used here –
'*...to add verisimilitude to an otherwise bald and*
unconvincing narrative.'
There are an extra ten points available if you can identify
the quote (above). In most cases, points mean prizes. In
this case they are merely an accumulation of self
satisfactory plaudits.

** In the next song there is also a 'points gaining'
reference; however, due to the particularity of its
occasioning, there is only a single favour available. Sorry!

SEVEN-POSTER BED

Here is another nonsense-song, sung to the tune of Manley Pier. It is therefore particularly good value if sung anywhere in Australia, to any Australians or in any of several Australian accents.

I've seen the natural devotion of the porpoise in the ocean.
I've seen an ostrich nearly lose its head
And I've seen a flying fox wear different coloured socks
But I've never seen a seven-poster bed.

I've had scorpions in my boots, heard a windbag play the flutes.
I've seen a coyote catch some catamoles.
*I've had **chiggers in my tea**** and a surprising kind of flea*
But I've never seen a bed with seven poles.

Now I've slept in good hotels and smelt funny kinds of smells.
I've travelled over valleys, hills and coasts.
I've tried every sort of bed, even hammocks overhead,
But I've never slept in one with seven posts.

So I think I'll change my plans and forget those big divans
And let them lie forever unbeknown;
For I think I must have read it, or someone might have said it,
"If you want a bed like that - then build your own!"

Chorus:

Seven-up, get 'em up! Seven-down, get 'em down!
Keep your long-johns buttoned-up behind.
If you cannot find a bunk, sell your soul - become a monk,
But keep the worms of discontent from off your mind.

(Thanks must be given to **Dickie Barr**, from **'Rattlin' Down'**, and to all-round entertainer and legendary Naval folk-singer, **Shep Woolley** for helping put the last two verses and the chorus into perspective.)

ROTATE YOUR CROPS

If you would like something on a more historical note, and certainly if entertaining academics, schoolmasters and the like, this song of the 'tomfoolery' genre would fit nicely into any situation.

The problem here is to sing it in a Cornish accent, or a Devon accent or a Worcestershire accent. The latter is probably best as it is easier. Besides, there will be other Worcestershire-type songs later - 'zo tiz praap'r youm git in a bit o' praaktiz, inn-it?!'

Jason Goodright bought a farm in 1443
And sold his business in the Town
To help to pay the fee
But he found he did not know
What crops to reap, what crops to sow
Nor which way round his farm would go,
In 1443.

"Rotate your crops." the Farmers said in 1443.
"Throw your weeds in the nettle-bed
"Before and after tea.
"Rotate your turnips and your wheat,
"The fallow for your cows to eat
"And thus their dung provides their meat,
"In 1443."

So Jason had his turnips dug in 1443.
He put his wheat into a jug
And danced around with glee.
He had some hay fetched from the shed

And tied the whole lot up with thread
And as he whirled it round his head
He fell and sprained his knee.
('ee warn't a p'ticl'r good varmer, warn't Jason!)

Chorus;
Rotate, gott'a rotate; rotate, gott'a rotate; rotate, gott'a
rotate.
Rotate yer crops with me.

SHOLTOs ON THE MOVE

Sholto's Irregular Naval Balloon Artillery (the Diehards),
or as they are more regularly known - The SINBADs - are
an ancient and venerable Regiment. Consisting entirely of
Officers, they have the peculiarity that - the higher the
rank, the less flamboyant the uniform becomes. Indeed,
very senior Officers wear sandals (an historical precedent)
instead of the more normal ballooning-boots.
Steeped in tradition, each Officer is hung about with
reminders of the SINBADs' glorious past: chopsticks from
the Chinese Wars, gharam-massala from the Indian Mutiny
(which, being in extremis, they took instead of snuff) and
miniature sand-bags to commemorate their finest hour
suspended above the Boer War.
A cry of *"Sand-bag!!"* normally accompanies any
meeting of two or more members of this illustrious
Battalion (reduced in the recent Ministry of Defence cuts)
and presages some pretty serious refreshment taking in the
nearest Lounge Bar (all, of course, in the interests of being
able to maintain equilibrium in the rarefied ether of a
soaring Basket).

The story below tells of a small boy wakened at midnight
to witness the departure of these Heroes, at some time late
into the second half of the 19th century. You should
picture the lad, rubbing sleep from his eyes and clad only
in a nightshirt, as he hangs onto the long skirts of his
mother. They are standing on an upstairs balcony of
wrought iron, of the sort only found in a foreign country.

Below them march the troops, almost glowing in the flicker-flames of burning torches, as they are thinly cheered by the town's populace.

The boy speaks in a soft treble; his Mother in a deep contralto.

Boy: *"Where are they marching tonight, Mother?*
Why are they striding away?
Who are those men with their faces so stern?
Where are they going today?"

Mother: *"Hush, Dear, remember this well.*
Though it is late, don't complain.
This is the story that one day you'll tell:-
'When the 'Sinbads' set out on campaign'."

Boy: *"Where are their muskets and swords, Mother,*
Or are they all ailing with pain?
For I see that each man, on his arm, is equipped
With a Gentleman's stout walking cane."

Mother: *"Hush, Dear, and cease to lament,*
For they have no wounds to anoint;
But a gun is no use to a 'Helium Vent'*
And a stick is a good thing to point."

Boy: *"Where are the Men of the Line, Mother?*
Where are the Soldiers to fight?
Where is the General astride of his horse?
Why are their numbers so slight?"

Mother: *"Hush, Dear, no Ranks will they send,*
No General, nor yet a Dragoon;
For how many Officers can you suspend
In a basket beneath a balloon?"

Boy: *"Why do they go to the War, Mother?*
What will they do to the Foe?
Who will be there on the left and the right?
What other Regiments go?"

Mother: *"Hush, Dear, the answer is plain;*
For they are of steady resource.
They go up. They come down.
Then they share their champagne (with)
*The bold 'Raz al Hamrah Light Horse'."***

Boy: *"Where's their accoutrement freight, Mother?*
Where is their long baggage-train?
With only a Stick and a Bucket of Sand
Their battle will soon be in vain."

Mother: *"Hush now, importunate child!!!*
Don't make a dance and a song.
When Sholtos go out to the Wars in the Wild,
They're never away very long."

(Written by: Helium Vent 1st Class the Notable Oropesa
Molgoggah-Fid-Sholto R101SM.)

Notes:
* Helium Vent: A rank equivalent to a Lieutenant
Commander. Normally referred to as a Helium Vent First

Class but, as there are no Second Class Helium Vents anyway, the abbreviation is acceptable in this case.
**Raz al Hamrah Light Horse: The Sholtos' 'Chummy' Regiment. Nothing much is known about this Force beyond the fact that they are quite as well established as the SINBADs; that they wear a splendid Hussar-type uniform in bright pink and that they drink nothing but champagne.

Perhaps it would be as well to point out that *'The Sinbads'* are an entirely fictitious Regiment, invented by a group of like-minded Adventurers who were working in the Middle East at the time. Aware of the sometimes strange and ritualistic 'traditions' rife in British Army Regiments' officers' messes, particularly during Formal Dinners, they decided to create their own off-the-wall Unit that could encapsulate all of these unlikely traditions and then some. They had their own uniforms made, wrote a history of *'The Die-hards'* and invented the most improbable conventions to be associated with them. As an example: during a Mess Dinner, should any infringement of the rules be even hinted at, anyone may shout *"Sand-bag!!"*; at which evocation all must stand on their chairs, place one foot on the table and echo the cry before draining the nearest glass. There is no point to this, it just happens. Such was the popularity of this concept that other like-minded folk, in a nearby establishment, invented *'The Raz-al-Hamra Light Horse'* in similar manner. There occurred one memorable (up to the point when all memories began to fail) night when both Regiments met up for the ultimate *'Guest Night'* at the *'Sinbads'* Mess. Special medals were awarded to the survivors.

Such occasions are redolent of the Expats' sense of fun, in a time when 'making your own entertainment' was of paramount importance.

It is what this book is all about.

[Note: The photograph on the title page shows Bernie in the uniform of a 'Sinbad' Helium Vent First Class (Senior); as indicated by the fact that he wears sandals instead of the more lowly ballooning boot - or - 'Kodiak mukluk'.]

DORSET IS BEAUTIFUL

The difficulty that immediately becomes apparent is that
this song has to be sung with a Dorset accent. No other
inflexion will quite do justice to the piece. Devon or
Worcestershire, although sounding similar, would merely
chip away at the verisimilitude extant in the inherent
veracity of the sentiment, to leave it wasted and
unsubstantial. A Welsh intonation could be tried but might
sound a bit stupid (not surprisingly). The tune is 'The
Nightingale'.

Dorset is beautiful, or so I've been told,
With creamy rice puddings and pots full of gold.
It's lovely in the summertime, as well I do know,
With your Darling in a dung-heap under ten foot of snow.

Dorsetshire Farmers are all well aware
That the average banana-skin, asleep in his lair,
When roused by the Oouzle Bird, of which you've heard
tell,
Will run-amok in the cabbage patch and jump down the
well.

Walking through the marigolds, a-drinking my tea,
Espying a rodent, I shouted with glee,
"I don't mind you ravaging my fine carrot bed
But don't lie there comatose, do press-ups instead."

My Sister's in the Cavalry. My Uncle's a Vet.
My Grandma breeds antelopes. My Father's in debt.
My Cousin is an idiot and, very sad to tell,
My Brother is a banana-skin down somebody's well.

So come down to Dorset and stay for a year.
If you treat us kindly, you've nothing to fear.
But beware of the banana-skins and the Oouzle Bird's peck
Or you'll go back to Eng-a-land a gibbering wreck.

For Dorset is beautiful, or so I've been told,
With creamy rice puddings and pots full of gold.
It's lovely in the summer time, as well I do know,
With your Darling in a dung heap under ten foot of snow.

THE BLOODY GOBBITS OF FLESH

This is a short but Epic Poem that has in the past held audiences spellbound, speechless and occasionally green (it must be hoped) with envy. It is the apogee of the Declaimer's art in which, aided by modulation, pause, inflection and tone, he can conjure up a vivid picture of the agonies of hand-to-hand combat.

It should be delivered in a thick Scots accent. The more genteel strains of 'Morningside', as intoned so graciously by **Dame Maggie Smith** in *'The Prime of Miss Jean Brodie'*, will be too soft to do justice to the raw animalism necessary for the performance. However, it is the perfect accent for the last line.

Introduction: (in normal voice)
 Picture the scene. As a rain-laden gale sweeps across lonely Scottish moors, the Battle is drawing to a close. Dark clouds, harbingers of the lost day, hurtle across a sky where black crows circle, in their hunt for carrion. Beneath them, cunning foxes skelter among the dead, bent on similar prey. The fighting is all but over; yet here and there a Warrior Chieftain still stands defiant as he seeks escape from the carnage. Our Hero, his bloody Claymore stilled for a moment, glares at the red-coated Enemy that encircles him as - - - (shift to Scots accent)

He faced them with defiance,
His sword was in his hand.
They circled and advanced a pace
To where he made his stand.

They threatened him with 'gert' long pikes
And halberds, sharp as knives,
As he with thrust and parry
Essayed to take their lives.

But sword and dirk against a pike
Nor halberd can prevail
And so, within an hour or two,
His strength began to fail.

A deadly blow, a scything slash
Drew forth a bloody spurt;
So down he fell with tendons cut
To struggle in the dirt.

They stabbed at him with knife and sword.
They hit him with nailed clubs
And, sticking skewers through his cheeks,
They dragged him through the shrubs.

His arms were broken and his legs
Were fractured in the fray,
For many were the wounds that he
Received that fateful day.

*(They slit his belly open and
His guts erupted forth,
With spleen and kidneys, bladder
And intestines south and north.

They reached inside the cavity
And grasping at a lung

They wrenched it from its very roots
And then ripped out his tongue.)*

His eyes gouged out, his ears tore off,
His skull and brain trepanned,
Oozing blood and gore;
(switch to Morningside accent)
It was not the day he'd planned!

(Note: The portion enclosed by (brackets) and annotated by a * at the beginning and at the end*, may be left out if the Performer is of a nervous disposition, or if it is felt that inclusion might make the audience sick. However, it should be remembered that it is a part of the whole and, as such, should be treated in like manner.)

FOR WHAT?

Should the Adventurer find himself trapped in that most uncertain of environs - the Nursery - (and it can happen), he will find this piece very handy.

It is one of the strange peculiarities about Parents, that they automatically assume other people will be as excited and happy at the prospect of *'playing with the Children'* as they themselves are forced to be.

It is not always the case with the Traveller, particularly if Nanny is away and he is forced to become an ersatz version of one of those mystical creatures.

'For What?' may be rated equally with:

"Hickery dickery doc, two mice ran up the clock.
The clock struck one but missed the other one."   - and with:

"Mary, Mary, quite contrary, how does your garden grow?
With silver bells and cockle shells and one absolutely
gargantuan holly-hock."

and serves to completely confuse the Little Darlings. Further, it may perhaps cause Mama to rescind the Sentence, allowing escape and freedom to ensue. However, it is noticeable that the Small People do find great fascination in the last two lines; often clamouring for a repeat performance

Simple-minded Cyril and Samarium the Seer
Sought the Slipper Serpent with sabre, sword and spear.
Several sorts of sable were saddled silently
But sadly Cyril saw them slope-off slyly to the sea.
Samarium made matters more than mildly mazarine,

*Meeting mostly Maharajahs, more than motley
Maharines.
A million mental Malacites were mentioned in the main,
Making mercenaries military madness to maintain.
This 'diagmatic' dialogue deserves a different death
From a day's decapitation as a danger to the deaf.
With dinosauric dignity we'll dance it down the deck
Where we'll tie heavy weights to its feet and throw it
overboard -
so that it drowns in the watery wastes of the South
Atlantic.*

(This was originally another of the exercises given to
Albert Kirk in an effort to improve his diction; but it
became such a popular little piece that it seemed a shame
to waste it after he no longer had need of its efficacy.
Consequently it was conscripted to the Nursery - much to
Nanny's chagrin.)

THE TALE OF ANNIE

Set to the well known tune of *'The Treshing Machine'*, this song is particularly effective when the Wanderer is called upon to sing at a Folk Club. It should be performed in the traditional 'Folkie' manner with eyes closed, one finger thrust into the ear and an expression of rapt concentration upon the face. It should also be sung through the nose, with every other line ending in the orthodox "-wah" of the genuine Folk-singer. For added authenticity, it might be appropriate to insert a nasal "Nya-a-ah" preceding the first word of each verse. Finally, wear a chunky-knit sweater, a 'fisherman's cap, a red and white spotted neck-a-chief and have a pewter tankard hanging by a leather strap from the belt or braces (or both, if complete safety is required). The last two lines of every second stanza and the last three at the end of the song should be spoken. To make life easier, these have been printed in **bold**.

Oh, list while I tell you a story quite true
Of poor little Annie, who fell in some glue.
They searched and they searched for her all through the night
But poor little Annie had sunk out of sight.

Chorus: (optional)
In the glue, in the glue;
Poor little Annie is way overdue.

She swam through the glue, so sticky and thick,
Till she got to the bottom, of brickety-brick.
She found a small hole and slid through with a shlurp

And saw that she'd landed in a very nice little apartment in the back streets of Montmatre, Paris, which was furnished very comfortably, for what appeared to be a not-inconsiderable sum.

(chorus, optional)

The Flat was so nice she decided to stay
And settled down quietly for the rest of the day,
But later that eve' came a knock at the door
And there stood a man with a carburettor.

(optional chorus)

"I've come for my lesson, O Mistress." he said.
He bowed to the floor, put her foot on his head.
"I've brought this inductor which I've had refurbished;
So shall we commence with lesson sixty-three in the course of bizarre sexual practices, at twenty five pounds per session, Monday to Friday, eight till ten?"

(You may put a chorus in here - if you like.)

Well, Annie was taken aback with surprise.
She could hardly believe her ears or her eyes.
She decided to do it, and quickly rebounded,
For twenty-five guineas. (not twenty five pound - Ed:)

(There is room for a chorus here. It is up to you.)

She stripped him. She whipped him. She bound him with chains.

She painted him with wood-preservative stains.
She supplied what he craved for to such an extent
That he cried as he left, "O Madam, Madam! Be mine!
Be mine!" But of course Annie refused, knowing that
she could make far more money where she was. She was
no fool.

(Penultimate chance for a chorus, tha' knows.)

But, sad to relate, our tale is not done;
For what can be said of her Dad and her Mum?
Because they've been searching for Annie so long
That all they can do now is, each year, drop another
birthday cake into the glue-vat and hope that it finds its
way to Annie; who does not care either way because she
is rolling in money - and is no longer in a sticky
situation.

(OK. Last chance for a..., well, you know what I mean – if
you must!)

PROSE AND SPEECH

It is more than likely, indeed highly desirable, that the Traveller will keep a Journal. It serves as a retrospective itinerary and a passable reminder, in later years, of his wanderings.

Many such Diaries can be extremely boring, being solely concerned with dates and times and movements. As **Peter Cook's** intro-dynamic character **E L Wisty** put it,

"They are so boring; they ought to be set as examination subjects for school children."

Such records will not read well unless a certain descriptive flair is incorporated, and in consequence might well be consigned to the pile of *'must read that someday'* books - that never are.

Eric Newby's collection, *'A Book of Travellers Tales'*, contains many fascinating and expressive pieces; but how many of these have been culled from otherwise uninspired narratives? The Voyager should try to include such gems to sprinkle through his otherwise bald yarn so they stand out like jewels on black velvet to any later reader. For himself, a word here and a phrase there will be enough to bring back the mental picture of the relevant episode but to the uninformed, the man who finds the account perhaps years later, the trick will not work. What is needed is good, solid prose that tells it like it was. This is not always easy to do and, like the 'party piece', requires practice.

It is all about words, using words, having fun with words, putting words next to other words and seeing how they turn out, finding new words, applying old words. It is about having: a love for your own language; an appreciation that it is the only one that can express itself so dramatically and succinctly; a feel for its timbre, its sound, its versatility; and it is about getting out there and doing it.

Mostly, however, the Venturer should pick a random point from his travels and try to describe it, looking beyond the commonplace to find that special facet that each possesses. He should not dwell overlong on the piece, for in brevity, well considered brevity, lies the fizz and sparkle of description. Or perhaps, if time hangs heavy, he should simply write his whimsy down. Either way he and his Record will benefit.

But before we get to that, how about some.......

INSTANT SHAKESPEARE

It began as a conversation in a Bar. The subject was
'Instant Shakespeare'. One of the collocutors was renowned
for his Shakespearean recitations and much sought after on
that score at Parties. The other was cognizant that what he
heard was not the genuine article but was impressed with
the performer's memory.
Then came the secret - **memory** was quite unnecessary.
All that was required was **method**.

To produce 'Instant Shakespeare' the rules are these:
1) Never start a sentence with anything other than a 'But',
'With', 'And', 'So', 'From', 'Though' - etcetera.
2) Always speak in slow and ringing theatrical tones, much
as the Actor/Manager of old was deemed to have done.
This will give you time to think.
3) Word repetition is useful but rhyme should only be used
in the last two lines.
4) Say anything that comes into your head, relevant or not,
provided it can in some way be connected to that which
precedes it. Digression is essential, but a final return to the
theme imperative.

So the challenge was given, that each should return to the
Bar that evening with a prepared piece; the first of these
was to be that cry, often heard at the scene of a hit-and-run
motor accident ....

DID ANYBODY GET HIS NUMBER?

Whereof did the fleeting dalliance,
With present mirthlessness and round alarum,
Thus escape that Justice bidden to the scene
And, without a measured brilliance -
That which measured ought to be,
Did cock a snook at our pair-fingered rage,
So do we ask the yeoman farmer in his turn,
The coppersmith and publican as well and
Even of the baser sort that do
In this environ make their trade,
Whether any, all or each of these,
Or each one in his turn, can with a will,
Yet willingly enough to let that will
The more than willing be, give us council
And converse upon the subject of the score,
Summation, reckoning or gross
Belonging to that miscreant equipe;
That might we, with right and justice in our hand,
Enter such advice upon the Seeking-persons of the Land.

As this is, perhaps, the first time that you have encountered
'Instant Shakespeare', it would be a kindness to explain
some of the words, tricks and stratagems that are extant in
the piece above.
(Gosh! this 'Instant Shakespeare' sure does get to one,
don't it?)

Whereof did the fleeting dalliance,
('dalliance': a type of 18th century horse-drawn 'buggy',
the sports-car of its day. 'fleeting' – going at a fair lick.)

With present mirthlessness and round alarum,
(angrily sounding his horn)

Thus escape that Justice bidden to the scene
(scarpered before the Police arrived)

And, without a measured brilliance -
That which measured ought to be,
(without stopping to argue the point)

Did cock a snook at our pair-fingered rage,
(ignored our proffered 'V'-sign)

So do we ask the yeoman farmer in his turn,
The coppersmith and publican as well and
Even of the baser sort that do
In this environ make their trade,
(we asked for witnesses from the local businesses and
street traders)

Whether any, all or each of these,
Or each one in his turn, can with a will,
Yet willingly enough to let that will
The more than willing be, give us council
And converse upon the subject of the score,
(whether any of them would be willing to tell us)

Summation, reckoning or gross
Belonging to that miscreant equipe;
(what was the number-plate of the vehicle)

That might we, with right and justice in our hand,
Enter such advice upon the Seeking-persons of the Land.
(so that we can do our duty and tell the Police
investigators.)

or: **"Did anybody get his number?"**

(Note: The four lines, *'Whether any, all or ....to....... the*
more than willing be' is a typical Shakespearian 'joke'
based on the words 'will and willing'; not very amusing to
us today but in the Bard's time had them rolling in the
aisles.)

Descriptive pieces need not be of any great moment,
nor of a particularly notable environ. Although useful for
comparison and continuity, a written depiction of, say, the
Taj Mahal would be purely repetitious of others'
renditions. Instead, look for simple things and describe
them. It is astonishing how much goes on very close to us
that we never notice.

BUSH

There is a Bush that grows before my window.
It is not a bushy Bush,
Nor indeed has it any discernible leaves.
It is really just a Bush made of stalks.
At the bottom it appears to be dead .
But this is an illusion as, higher up,
It proliferates with green branchettes
Reaching toward the sky.
The 'green' is light and yellowy in colour and
Each stalk has at its extremity miniature florets attached.
These tiny flowers attract many insects.

First there are Hornets.
Some are yellow with red stripes.
They look more akin to
Elongated wasps than true hornets
And are not seen very often.
Occasionally a Great Hornet arrives.
He is maroon in colour, with a single, broad, yellow stripe
Across his abdomen.
He looks mean and very unhappy.

Great Hornets are not nice creatures.
A sting from one of these will paralyse a limb
And cause it to become hugely inflated.

Most common of all are Yellow-ochre Hornets.
They fly with their long legs dangling and their tails
cocked up.
This gives them a sinister air, and rightly so.
Their sting is akin to the application of 2000 volts.
They like to cling to the lintels of doors and surrounding
walls.
From this position, in order to take to the air,
They simply let go –
Fall –
Deploy wings and swoop away.
Unlucky is he who exits as they make this manoeuvre.
On meeting with such an obstacle,
The enraged creature will attack for all his worth.
Normally he stings at the neck.
I do not like Yellow-ochre Hornets.

Then there are the Ants.
There are Big Blacks and Little Blacks,
Reds and Oranges.
The speed at which they run up and down the stalks
Is really quite astonishing.
They spend an enormous amount of time doing this
And scarcely stop for food.
But they are sociable creatures and
Always pause for a moment to greet a friend or colleague
As they pass.

What are they looking for?
Why all this expense of energy?
What do they achieve?
It is all very odd.

A small cloud of tiny insects, fruit flies perhaps,
Hovers above the Bush.
Occasionally they land in its upper branches.
Others fly circles and spirals in
The heart of the plant itself.
Meanwhile, I look beyond the Bush
Towards the small segment of Ocean that the window
frames.

I watch a slow sailing boat go past
On a steady course.
At least he seems to know
Where he is going.

This is a piece of prose. It is **not** a poem. I have presented it to appear as though it is a poem - but it isn't. It's a piece of poem-shaped prose. It is what passes for poetry these days and tends to be produced by those who are too idle to do the thing properly.

Poetry is very difficult to write. It requires structure and flow and follows complicated rules. It may also contain meter and rhyme; there are many different forms. It is not enough to write a piece of prose, shape it to look like verse and call it Poetry. That is cheating, and it is fraud. There are too many people doing that today – and they are getting away with it!

The 'poem' (below) is the piece of prose (above) but arranged to look like a poem in the foolish misapprehension that people will mistake it for such and heap plaudits upon the author. Be warned! Centre-text alignment, the splitting up of lines, an absence of capital letters and punctuation – does not a poet make.

this is a piece of prose
*it is **not** a poem*
i have presented it to appear as though it is a poem –
but it isn't
it's a piece of poem-shaped prose
it is what passes for poetry these days
and tends to be produced by those
who are too idle to do the thing properly
poetry is very difficult to write
it requires structure and flow
and follows complicated rules
it may also contain meter and rhyme
there are many different forms
it is not enough to write a piece of prose
shape it to look like verse and call it poetry
that is cheating, and it is fraud
there are too many people
doing that today
and they are
getting away
with
it!

POLITICAL SPEECH, FOR ANY PARTY ON ANY OCCASION

In days gone by, when filling in an application form for your first Passport, it was necessary to have as counter-signatory one of the following:
Doctor, Clergyman, Bank Manager, Justice of the Peace, Officer in Her Majesty's Armed Forces, Solicitor and the like; all of whom had spent long years in study and examinations to reach their position of trust and authority. Incongruously, the list also included – Member of Parliament; whose only required qualification was *'the ability to lie convincingly'*.
Now, I do not know if anyone actually listens to these people but they seem to have a way of talking without saying anything of substance. It may be that they are frightened that, if they should speak substantially, they will be held to account for what they have (or haven't) said.

This piece is for them.
They should need nothing more.

"When I first, many years ago, started my way in life, it was with hope that I stepped forward along the road to great and better things.
Little did I realise that I would be here, now, speaking to you tonight.

Let me say, as I have said many times before, that even though the times may change - and they do - there is no-

*one who wishes more fervently than I that, leaving
aside all our differences, even though we tend to forget, we
should stand firm.
Let me just say this.*

*Many of you here tonight, no matter who you may be (and
where would we be without you?) should search in your
hearts; and indeed many of you may have wondered - as I
have.....   Well, look no further.*

*These are not mere empty assurances for, as this sceptre'd
Isle goes forth, and I speak from the bottom of my heart,
without fear of contradiction, the facts are these:*

*There has never been and perhaps will never be again,
despite what the critics may say, - - and it is indeed a fine
thing - for who are we to scoff?
There is no doubt that we, in our stumbling way, when all
hope was lost, gazed forward and marched toward new
horizons.*

*So, what can we look for?
Where will it end?*

*I shall speak, as I always do, bluntly, forthrightly and, with
no fear of tomorrow's truth, squarely within the limits of
the factual encompassment.*

*And so, with unshakeable faith, let us pull together. Let us
not be afraid; for who would dare to deny it?*

And finally, let me be brief.

As we can see about us every day, let me assure you that, even if there was the slightest grain of truth, the question remains.

All things being equal, I am honoured - nay - humbled, and so I pledge my word to you all."

The second of the pieces from the 'Instant Shakespeare Challenge' concerned the inability of one guest at a Tea Party to ensure that the Pot went, as the Navy has it, 'round the Buoy'. Thus his neighbour may have asked...

*WILL YOU PASS THE ****** TEA!*

Thus does the casket of the rarest vapour
Sit with easy grace upon the damask coverlet
And, as given often to the multitude,
Wait with patience to enrich our essences;
So, with the staying of thy hand,
Shall the routed bush, that e'en its leaves
Doth offer up to that fair muse,
Bethought by many with injustice
To be the one necessity of life itself,
Those that are enriched by flaming orb
And gentle zephyr rain, do thrust
And thrust again to notoriety,
That, e'er picked and pressed afore,
Yet shall they a sweet diffusion make,
A nectar for the stilling of unquiet souls;
So will it cast its thoughts to suicide
If gainful use be not its favoured lot.

Thus, with entreaties sweet
And words of fairest enterprise,
Does this poor mortal, whose bones
Are even now with tarnished toil ensnared,
Fathom out the basic meanings

Of a scant and seeming unexpected ruse.
Shall not the chariots of the fairest Gods,
That are by Jupiter and Neptune early spurned,
Holding to the knave that wishes such
A wonton and ignoble act
And feign to share the garner of our land,
Smite with rings of fire
That miser of the honey'd draught?

But stay!
Reverse your plenteous spirit.
Suffer not an envy to emerge
But, with good grace and sober recompense,
Reveal to us in tangent order
That which thou dost guard,
As here described before;
And then with carefree holder-ness
Receive again once more.

And I reckon that that is about as good as it gets.

Here's an idea: if you are a Scholar (as school-children are designated these days) take it into your English Literature class and see what the Teacher has to say about the piece.

Later in the book you will find some *'Instant Robbie Burns'*, with which you may confuse even more people.

There are times when a handful of Voyagers, Adventurers and like-minded individuals meet, perhaps at a Pub for the week-end, to entertain each other with yarn and song, and of course the occasional drink. These are the Magic Times when the evening is enlivened by Ditty, Wit and Music – preferably played without amplification, so unnecessary in anything but a giant venue.

One such evening held, round the table, a group of Adventurers whose combined achievements bordered on the unbelievable. They were as diverse, yet as unified as could be imagined; but it was a Company that one seldom has a chance to meet.

Here they are:

At the head of the table sat *'The Fiddler'*, whose expertise in that particular field had won him the accolade of being sought out to play on stage with the world's greatest Jazz violinist, **'Stephane Grappelli'**. In an earlier period of his life, he had been a Colour Sergeant in the Royal Marines, a mountaineer and a renowned sailor and yachtsman.

Next to him was the man, also an ex-Royal Marine, who had made the longest, unsupported and un-sponsored, solo canoe voyage in history – from the Russo-Finnish boarder, down the coast of Norway, around the entire coastline of the Baltic and all the way to Spain.

Then came an American who had emulated **Captain Joshua Slocomb**; building his own boat by hand (a replica of Slocomb's **'Spray'**) and had sailed it around the world, exactly following his hero's epic voyage.

Surrounding the other end of the table was *'The Gunner'*. This mountain of a man had followed that trade in the Royal Navy, during which service he had also run for the *'Field Gun'* (the world's most dangerous sport) as 'heavy end', the preserve of only the strongest of men. He was also reckoned to be the Navy's number-one Mountaineer and had, in his time, held the Far East Fleet Heavyweight boxing championship. He could also declaim the classical Poets, faultlessly and for as long as he needed.

Alongside him sat an *'Artist and Sculptor'*, whose carved-wood ship's figurehead was currently being exhibited at the Royal Society. He had sailed across the Atlantic in the replica ***'Golden Hind'*** and had lived for two years in Canada, in a log cabin that he had built on the back of a 1932 fire engine; learning from the Eskimos the secrets of their Art.
Having saved from destruction the only existing example of a 19th century *'Gentleman's straight-stemmed Yacht'*, he was in the process of rebuilding her.
He was also a virtuoso pianist and one of only two people known to play all manner of Jazz on the Concertina.

Another concertina virtuoso was sitting next to him and was *'News Correspondent to a National tabloid Newspaper'*. He was also a sport diver, song writer and expert on the ever-so-difficult 'Duet' concertina, on which he too played the Jazz.

A *'Racing-driver'* occupied the adjoining chair. His distinction was to have been the youngest Commentator at the famed *Shelsley-Walsh Hill-climb* circuit; the only man brave enough to drive the monstrous *Fiat 'Mephistopheles'* world-speed record car up it; and the fact that whatever car he raced, just because *he* had raced it, immediately tripled its value.

Sitting quietly next to him was a *'Clearance Diver'* of legendary repute in the Royal Navy. No-one really knew just what these shadowy figures were about but they did know that it was dangerous work, something to do with bomb-disposal and parachuting and that this particular one had been twice decorated by *Her Majesty the Queen*.

And finally, taking up the last seat was a man who had started from the humblest beginnings to rise in the entertainment world to become a *'Household Name'*. He had already achieved his long-held ambition to 'have a thousand acres and a million pounds' and was now seeking out derelict horses, that he rescued and nurtured to turn into Show Champions.

This then was the gathering, for one night only, of such united souls.

Later, some went this way and some went that, and some went out at closing time to their tents, pitched in the landlord's paddock, where they spent a restful night. Then, next morning........

CAMP

The campsite looked like something out of 'Scott of the Antarctic', in that hard New Year's winter weather. Snow had fallen heavily and the fitful wind, sometimes racing flat across the tree tops, at others soft as a whisper's caress, had heaped it into drifts around the tents that humped the small field like fallen warriors on the Retreat from Moscow.

Half hidden, they lay as miniature mountain peaks, drifted high in the passes and exposing ice-clad faces to the gale. On one high snow-field, cracks began to appear and a tremor heralded the small beginnings of an avalanche as, with a rip of sound, the whole of one white-powdered slope bowed outward, parted and revealed from the shadow within, a tousle-headed beard supporting two bleary eyes and a sharp nose. Letting forth a fume of steamy vapour, the mask split asunder in a majestic yawn and looked upon the scene with quiet contentment.

"Come on, Shipmates. Rise and shine. 'Tiz a beautiful day out here an' the snow's only light. Tiz proper 'andsome!"

The words issued from the maw in a deep bass that penetrated to the further reaches of the paddock and engendered groans and grumbled comments from the occupants of the other tents.

The canopy trembled, shook and finally convulsed as the giant corpus of the speaker emerged into the crisp morning air, clad in a woollen shirt, comfortably worn but baggy cellular undershorts and climbing boots.

Clutching a bottle of rum in one sizeably tattooed paw, the giant (for so he seemed) stretched to his full six foot eight and two hundred and fifty pounds before shambling purposefully over to the nearest tent. He grasped the top of

the front pole and shook it with gentle insistence
until the snow slid off in sheets and the fabric quivered.

"Wakey, wakey, wakey! Heave-ho, 'eave-'o, 'eave-'o!
Show a leg, show a leg, show a leg!
Tot mugs to the fore.
Present yourselves to that fresh, clean Devon air."

Then he began to sing, in that way that only those who
cannot – do.

"If you're talking of your Rum
"You're drinking two and one.
"Chiefs and POs get it 'neaters'.
"But your stomach must be tough
"When the sea is getting rough
"And you've had a greasy dinner from the heaters.
"For it's Rum, Rum, Rum,
"Fill my belly with that Rum.
"You can keep your French Vermouth
"Just fill my hollow tooth
"With that wonderful elixir called Rum."

As the song progressed, with little regard for musical
notation or key, the animated earthquake moved about the
camp causing each shelter to shiver and shake until hands
reached out from under the flysheets with mug, cup or
glass. Each received its morning 'tot' and withdrew into
the comparative snugliness of the interior.
Meanwhile, the odd comment was heard,

"Cheers, Gunner. What's the weather like out there?"

"By! Was that some 'crack' last night!"
"Yurr! Whom got moi boots?"
"Sharing a tent with Bos'n is like sleeping under the lee of a cliff."
"Why do you say that, Diver?"
"Well, do you remember coming back to the campsite after the Pub last night?"
"Er, no. But do tell us....."

And so on.
With the rum-issue complete, his own mug charged, and in a voice not unused to rising above the din of six-inch gunfire, the colossus lifted his vessel high and roared,

"Gentlemen, the Queen!"

Came the muffled reply from within each and every tent,

"The Queen - God bless her!"

.....and all drank.

ROBIN OF SHERWOOD

Another descriptive piece, produced to combat the speech impediment of that poor, afflicted lad in *'HMS Blake'*, soon found favour as part of the Act of an old shipmate and one of our *'Contemporary Entertainers'* – namely – **Shep Woolley** – the renowned Naval Troubador.

It has been mooted that the Goodness of Robin Hood used to be disputed by the good boot-sellers who sold fruit for the loot that he found on his route, though the gout in his foot produced doubt that a faerie ferry was a very merry wherry where a jolly barrow of berries could be borrowed tomorrow.

So he took a look at a cook-book and hooked a crook from the nook of a brook where he was hiding, being frightened of the lightning, after stealing some whitening which belonged to a throng of long gong-bongers among whom were some strong wrong-doers, one called Wong.

He then went to an eating-meeting with some fleeting Heating Engineers who gave him a greeting while pleating their cloth; though the sloth of a moth had had enough of the stuff.

After running a while, he came to a stile where he spewed up some bile in a pile on a tile, while pale quail in the kale sent up a wail in the heart of the dale, that they'd failed.

So, when it got dark, he walked back through the park saying,

"Hark the dog bark." - - which it did!

FISHDISH

Probably one of the most successful aspects of Publishing concerns the production of Cookery Books. They make eminently suitable presents, gladly accepted, and yet, page for page, are perhaps the most seldom read of all volumes. It takes an especially dedicated cook to assemble all the ingredients designated in the recipe, following the instructions to produce a dish that even slightly resembles the accompanying Colour Plate.
It also requires considerable application and time; time that may be more usefully spent in other achievements.

But, profitable as these journalistic endeavours are, perhaps there is room for such a one here - though one that will not tax the Reader too heavily either in pocket or duration.

('Fishdish' is especially recommended for use by the Traveller, who will have little room in his Kit for the more complicated accoutrements of the culinary art.)

This is a really simple, tasty meal that requires absolutely no skill, little knowledge beyond what is written here and the minimum of time expenditure. You can make the execution of this recipe as complicated or as simple as you wish or as your abilities, aspirations and hunger dictate. Either way, there is little that can go wrong and the end result remains delicious.

You will need the following ingredients:
        A handful-and-a-half of rice (or macaroni)
        About a pint of water

A half-size tin of mackerel or, if you are
feeling solvent, salmon
An egg-cup-full of olive oil, sunflower oil, butter,
margarine or ghee
A little salt
A tea-spoon-full of ground black pepper.

And here's how you do it:
Put the salt in the bottom of a medium size saucepan, or a
small one, or whatever receptacle you elect to cook in – a
mess-tin, perhaps. Shake it around for a bit and see the
pretty patterns that are formed.
When you have finished doing that, pour in the water (if it
is hot water, then you will not have to wait so long on the
cooking) and add the rice (or macaroni, if that's what you
are using).
Put the pan, or whatever container you have chosen (but
not a Bakelite dish – Dickie Barr!) onto a high heat until
the water boils, then reduce the heat slightly to stop it
boiling over, yet to keep it bubbling fiercely. (Much the
same result can be achieved by leaving the heat turned up
to max and blowing constantly onto the boiling froth – a
good tip but rather time consuming.)
When all the water has been absorbed by the rice
(macaroni), it is cooked.
Now comes the easy part.

Add the half-tin of mackerel/salmon
Add the oil/butter/ghee/etc (whichever)
Stir it around thoroughly and then add the pepper.

Stir again (or add the pepper with the other stuff and
only stir once) and scoop it all out into whatever dish that
you intend out of which to eat it (grammatically correct).
I prefer to eat straight out of the pan as it saves on the
washing up; an important consideration if you are in a tent
or a small boat. However, if you wish to be traditional, a
Bakelite dish would be an admirable container –
particularly if you happen to be an Admirable.

Now scoff.
Delicious, ain't it?

There are other things you can add or substitute. They are:
       Curry powder, Tabasco, honey,
       Which-ever-spice-you-want-it-to-taste-of,
       Tomato pure', soya sauce, mushroom ketchup - and -
       Either: Tuna, Sardines, Pilchards, Herrings-in
(tomato sauce) or any other tinned fish. Kippers are
especially good.
You could also substitute Corned Beef, Frankfurters, Spam
etc but that is a different recipe called 'MEATDISH'.

Finally, always do your stirring with a twig or other
wooden article, particularly if using a non-stick pan. This
saves the food feeling gritty due to the scraped-off bits of
metal, or plasticy as a result of scouring the non-stick-
stuff.

PS. As a special treat, mix in a large spoonful of
mayonnaise just before eating. Don't worry about the
cholesterol. If this is the sort of food you are living on, you
need every bit of it you can get.

MEASURE FOR MEASURE

Consider this:

Oil, produced in 'barrels', is sold as litres of petrol; yet we reckon car-economy in miles per gallon.

Height is measured in metres, depth in fathoms, distance in kilometres and sea-miles; length is in inches, space in square feet and volume in cubic metres.

Land can be purchased in acres and hectares both.

Racetracks are in furlongs.

Ships are measured in feet and tons and their lading in tonnes (whatever they are – I thought they were fish).

Grain comes in bushels; beer in kegs, pins and hogsheads, yet it is sold in pints.

Otherwise fluid is referred to by its own ounce, which is quite different from that used in cookery, where one can also use 'spoonfuls' – flat or heaped.

We, ourselves, are weighed in stones.

Cigarettes are sold in twenties; Port in pipes, eggs in dozens, rags in bales and herrings in kips.

Steel comes in rolls, paper in reams, contraceptives in threes but wedding cakes are produced singly.

Income is reckoned in pounds sterling, deficits in dollars, with a yen for marks.

Air pressure is in bars - - as is beer.

Steam is in pounds per square inch and vacuum in inches of mercury.

Time and committees are both represented by minutes and arrows are weighed in pence. (Yes, they are!)

Ships proceed in knots, as do sailors (or, in the case of being abroad, in lines – across the road) – it's what they do.

Gold comes in troy.

Electricity, provided in kilowatts, produces energy in therms; whereas power is measured in horses, and horses in strings (priced in guineas).

Fahrenheit, Centigrade and Celsius are all different temperatures (Fahrenheit being the hottest).

Heat is produced by coal or gas, which are quantified in hundredweight and Marks.

Animals come in flocks, herds and prides; rain in cats and dogs and snow in flurries.

In the Tour de France, riders are measured in cycles per second - which hertz.

Yet nobody knows how many yonks there are in an aeon – and we still sell sand by the shovelful.

-o0o-

Remembering the usefulness of the Party Piece in
social circles around the world, it is advisable to have a
collection of recitations, songs and such like ready for any
occasion. As previously stated, an amusing rendition could
make all the difference between the Irish Linen sheets in
the Guest Bedroom and the sleeping-bag on a mattress in
the Hall; and between the,

"Thank you for coming; have a safe journey back."
and the much more promising,
*"Do stay for a few more days. My Daughters come back
from University tomorrow."*

(If this is followed by, *"I have to go away for a week, but
the keys to the 'Porche' are by the door to the Pool-patio;
do use any or all of them as you see fit."* - then so much
the better.) [This is known as 'the Ultimate Grip'. (see below)]

A 'Grip' is the partaking of freely offered hospitality by
members of the Hosting Country, normally when one of
Her Majesty's Warships visits a port whilst 'going
foreign'. The verb, 'to grip' is to avail oneself of that
hospitality and may be declined thus:
*'I grip; he grips; we will have been gripped; they would
have been about to have been gripping.'*
'The Ultimate Grip' involves the acquisition of food,
booze, accommodation, female company, a swim, fast cars
and spending money - - all for free; with a lift back to the
ship by chauffeur-driven limousine, a 'dolly bird' on each
arm, just in time for 'turn too' in the morning.'
Ah, Jack, such dreams!

One absolute essential is to have the answer to that
most devastating of questions,
*"Would you like to give the 'Reply on behalf of the
Ladies', after dinner this evening?"*
Whatever form this type of question assumes, it presages
the fact that the Guest will have to get up on his feet, clear
his throat, have a sip of water and launch into 'A Speech'.

Now, to give a really good speech, a great deal of time
must be spent in researching the occasion/person/event
about which it is to be given. Perhaps, by the very nature
of *'he for whom this book is written'*, no such interlude
will have been forthcoming and disaster will loom,
frowning, in the distance.

Fear not! Here, below, is the answer to the problem; a
universal panacea to be taken, seized upon, assimilated and
made his own. With the odd word inserted here, or
reference there, it is the **'Speech for All Occasions'**.
Indeed, it could even be used by the Errant Politician, in
place of his particular offering earlier in the book; although
that piece is simpler, uses more facile wordage and is
perhaps more suited to his intellect – and it's shorter.
But, worry not about the After Dinner Speech's efficacy. It
has been tested on more than one occasion – and it works.
On one notable occurrence, it was given at a Military Mess
Dinner.
The assembled officers became divided, naturally, into
three identifiable groups:

Older and more Senior Officers, who dozed comfortably,
only stirring as the Port came round again, and made

acquiescent mumblings at certain natural pauses in the dissertation.

(One Senior officer was once asked by the charming lady sitting next to him why he passed the Port to his left. His reply, *"Because I expect to get it back from my starboard beam!"*)

Middle Seniority and Staff Officers, who looked at one another in astonished query, but then nodded with the occasional, *"Hear, hear!"* just in case someone might see them being mystified by what was being said; 'coz that would never do for a 'Staaffie'.

Junior Officers, who had probably diverted the Port-train (decanters riding on wheeled, silver trucks for ease of passing up and down the table) into a siding of their own making; who thumped the board and cheered loudly at every 'point' made by the Speaker, and generally enjoyed themselves in the way Junior Officers are supposed to.

[As a Senior Officer said, to a Junior Officer, before dinner, "I hope you are going to behave yourselves this evening."   The Junior replied, "Yes, Sir, - - *badly!*"]

So, each of the three groups came away having acquired something from the occasion:

Seniors – a doze;

Staff O's – kudos;

Juniors – the chance to let off steam.

All were happy. All was well; and the Guest had acquitted himself quite wonderfully.

AFTER DINNER SPEECH (for all occasions)

It is not often that one, such as I, is given the opportunity
*of addressing such an **august** company, even if it is...........*
what month is it?
*However, the opportunity **has** been presented; I **am** here;*
*and I **shall** proceed.*

One should, it is true, prepare oneself a worthy plaudit for
such an occasion – an occasion so beset by the larger
standards that the caution exercised must be of conjecture,
not peremptory skill.

Therefore, with that in mind and without further respite,
without prevarication or delay,
delay that could cause doubt within - - without doubt;
***within** that doubt and **without** doubting the delay,*
*I shall doubtless **not** delay - but proceed.*
I shall, indeed, proceed; with no need for frills or foibles,
no fripprtty-frolls and folderolls
But proceed concisely and directly - - - onward.

Given the facts and the import thereof, and
notwithstanding the loss of any ordinary gain, we must, I
believe, stand firm.
We should not bow before the blatant importunitism of
pessimistic rhetoric,
nor should we deliver ourselves to the baser wanderings of
a nether intellect.
May we not rather say,

*"**Be gone!**" to the insignificant ramblings of the so-
called 'softer insight'?*
Should we not ejaculate,
*"**Away with you!**" to wasteful opulence – and declare,*
*"**Farewell forever!**" to analytical conjecture?*

*For, what ambiguity can ever replace the morass to which
we are all subject?*
*What senseless object can defer to half completed, half
rejected badinage?*
Where is the light of true peremptory judgement?
*And - has the objectivity of ascendant lambast left these
shores for ever? - I hear you ask.*
For these are 'wide' questions, to which I would reply....
Certainly not!!

But I shall speak bluntly, as I always do.
*Concisely and bluntly - for, with the knowledge that the
future holds the store and the past is but a garner-ground
for litigious sighs, we may for ever rely upon the one true
greatness of ascendant presence that lights the way before
us into the steely night.*
*There is nothing in the book of life that gives a finer
meaning.*
*There is no 'endroit' (that's yer actual French) that
shelters our longing from a disappointing fullness.*
*There is no form or spirit that can protect our inner
actions from another proximity.*

*We must march forward to dance in the light of that
semblance which alone sheds all pretence of ignorance –*

and never – ever - desist until that action has totally
fulfilled its potency.
For, if we do - then there shall be no alternative, - no
escape, - no safety in the recollection of tomorrow and no
heart-felt murmuring of a cherished fortune.

There lies the way.
There before us in a thousand lightless skies, stretching
further than our wanderings dare suggest.
We must reach out, grasp, struggle, overcome, subdue and
finally sanctify this brilliant antecedent of our hearts.
Then, and only then, may we find ourselves suspended in
the major plane and shriven to our end.

But what, we must ask ourselves, is the connection between
this cataclysmic sufferance and the feast that we have just
enjoyed?
Are we to liken it to the myths remembered only in the
unresponsive corners of a nether intellect?
If so, why pause for reaction?

No. I'm sorry. I'll do that bit again.
If so, why? - _(pause for reaction.)_

Where is the relevance of such untrammelled facings when
imposed upon the whole morass of fragmented ambiguity?
And who on earth saw **that** one coming?
These are also questions – not so wide, it is true – but
questions none the less.

*Perhaps the answer lies in the words penned by that
finest of all Scottish Romantics – 'Nobby' Burns – whose
cousin, 'Rabbie' achieved no little fame, or so I am led to
believe.
Who can forget his immoral lines upon the subject?
There is no need to repeat them here, of course, for we all
know them so intimately and well.
Are they not seared into the very fibres of our memories?
Do they not run – tripping, skipping, helter-skelter, lighter
than the gossamer itself – through our very beings?
No?*

*Well, maybe for the sake of the youngsters, perhaps just a
few lines from this, his most celebrated work – which, I
think you will agree, says it all:*

(assume a Scots accent:)

*Aye, awa' the Feemell graws
An' follows doon the Glen a-mair.
Nokht yer wee Akhrooder-mor
That, bleedin', falls a-neath the Hare.
Shno' the brikht fair limpid pool,
Shnae the Brackle-mundie's grin,
Brought to few yon Kirkle-grue
That beats the braggart breast within.
Beware the Wimprill-lassie, Mon!
Keep yer Breekhters twixt yer knees;
Or else the Feemell-trokht will come
An' fairly give yer Loure a squeeze!*

Surely, it is a good thing that we move-on every couple of years!

-o0o-

THE IMPOSSIBLE TASK

It all depends on the audience really; this piece can be done quite straight but the ending would have to be changed to:

"That only he could do it."

It has to be a fairly serious minded collection of people to warrant that drastic step, however.

Better by far is to render it in ringing tones, similar to the Actor/Manager of old, using grand and expansive gestures and in a *'Voice'*; as so admirably demonstrated by *Albert Finney* in the film *'The Dresser'*, when he delivered the devastating line,

"STOP THAT TRAIN!!!"

This initial 'grand manner' can gradually give way to the more clipped and precise technique of pseudo Shakespeare -

(as performed by *Peter Sellers'* impression of *Lawrence Olivier* in the part of *Richard III*, declaiming the words of *The Beatles'* *'Hard Day's Night'*; have you heard it? Quite marvellous!)

Physical enhancement to the monologue may be found during this phase by turning the knees inwards, dropping one hip, raising the opposite shoulder in a hunch and curling up that arm to the chest, fingers pointing floor-wards.

Move on then to slide into a Devonshire and then a Cornish accent before descending at the end into a full blown **Robert Newton** (as Long John Silver).
The last line should be said 'straight', in a normal voice.

Over the years this recitation has been performed in such diverse places as: the Submarine that sank **'the Belgrano'**; the Field Hospital at Red Beach during the Falklands War (and, later, at the end of an interview for News at Ten, with **Michael Nicholson** and **Brian** *'I counted them all out and I counted them all in'* **Hanrahan**, along with the late **Jeremy Hands**, who we all miss so much); at Rosie's Bar after the Monaco Grand Prix; in the *'Grand Bazzar'* at Istanbul (where no-one understood it but enjoyed the 'show') and at 900 feet before parachuting from a Hercules transport aircraft off the Channel Islands (don't ask!).

Isn't it amazing the things we get up to?

They said that it could not be done;
They said it was impossible.
They said, no man, however strong,
Could do what was not possible.
They said that many men had tried
In every way they knew
And, though they tried, they all had failed
This Thing, so hard to do.

He said that he did not believe
It was so very hard.
He said that he would strive and then
This Thing he would retard;
For was there not a tiny seed
In every English Heart
That, nurtured with the 'will-to-win',
Could form a greater part
And grow, with care, like English Oak,
Its roots thrust deeper yet,
Its branches spread and leaves extend,
Until the Task was met?

And should this seed of Courage grow,
Along with Gross Endeavour,
It should eclipse the baser tasks
'Till they are gone for ever.

For Man, no matter where he is,
No matter who he be,

Can rise again and overcome
And do the greatest deeds;
And, when he's strived and gained that part
Where Heroes always stood,
He'll count himself with Greater Men
And join their Brotherhood.

And so he said that he would try
This Thing to overcome
And strive with all his might and main
Until his Task was done.

They said that it could not be done.
They said that he would rue it,
But he faced the challenge and he found - -

He couldn't bloody do it!

A MEMORABLE REPAST

Occasionally, in his travels about the World, the Explorer may well be invited to partake of a Local Dish, generously provided by his Host or other acquaintance. But be warned, all may not be quite as straightforward as it seems.

The Nokahdar (Captain) of the Arabic Bhoum (Dhow*) invited us to sit upon the deck and enjoy his hospitality; but first he switched on a giant television-set, showing scenes of the desert, apparently filmed in a snow or sand storm.
As this was behind us anyway, it scarcely mattered. The music that accompanied the piece was long and intricate and appeared to consist of a maximum of five half-notes which were repeated at random, but all to the infectious rhythm of the drums.

After some desultory conversation concerning the welfare of his and our Families, and the price and efficacy of a new Toyota 'pick-up', a plastic mat was brought in and put upon the deck before us. Various dishes containing foodstuffs were placed thereon and we were invited to repose ourselves in a half-crouch, half-sit, half-kneel kind-of attitude, neatly spaced about the periphery.
Our Host then commenced to reverently ladle a thin, gray gravy over the central platter of rice and then plumped various pieces of meat-bound bones upon it. Then the head of the goat - for that is what we believed the meat to have been - boiled goat - was placed in the middle of the dismembered animal, sitting atop the rice mound, the tongue lolling from between its bared teeth.

*Ali Hamdan was in paroxysms of suppressed
laughter, engendered by a glance from our own Captain.
We all looked at our feet and forced ourselves to become
solemn as the occasion demanded.*

*Salad was prepared by squeezing half-limes over a
melange of coarsely chopped and venerable lettuce, onions
and green peppers and dumping great handfuls of the stuff
on the cloth in front of each guest. Dates were similarly
distributed.*
*There were also the crispened carcasses of dead fish
available on a side plate.*

*We commenced to eat, our Host taking enormous handfuls
of rice, meat, fish, dates and salad and cramming them
wholesale into his mouth.*
*We, on the other hand, but not <u>with</u> the other hand,
practised 'court-eating', the requirements of which limit
food residue to an area bounded by the middle knuckle of
each finger.*

*Halfway through the repast, we were joined by a man
dressed simply in a singlet and a 'wizzar' (a cloth wrapped
around the loins), who proceeded to wrench open the
goat's skull and deposit pieces of its adhering flesh among
the detritus of the main dish.*
*I had never before seen a man prizing out a goat's brain
with its own jaw-bone; using the blackened teeth to saw
through the tough bits. But this he did and offered us the
excavated mush as a delicacy.*

The Guests having refused this, with all thanks and gratitude, our Host consumed it himself - with obvious relish.
We were thankful that the eyes had seemingly been left out of the feast.

The meal was completed with large quantities of fruit that we were urgently encouraged to consume in their entirety; after which we retired to another part of the deck to watch the Nokahdar smoking a cigarette.

* A stitched-together, wooden, motor-driven, sailing, cargo boat indigenous to the Arabian coastline and sporting a lateen sail. The best ones are hand-built on the beach at Sur – south-west down the coast a bit from Muscat, in Oman.

-o0o-

FROM WITHIN

Travel provides the Wanderer with plenty of opportunity
to ponder the Measures of Life and equal opportunity to
write on such related subjects.
Train journeys are particularly efficacious in this respect,
perhaps the more so because of the sympathetic rhythm of
the wheels' thrum.

Expeditions to be commended are: The Blue Train from
Johannesburg to Cape Town, the Observation Car ride
between Inverness and the Kyles of Lochalsh on the West
Coast of Scotland, and the short trip from Plymouth to
Calstock in Devon.
(The Orient Express is perhaps the ultimate train-journey
but it is murderously expensive and, therefore, hardly
contributive to straight thinking nor, even,
recommendation).

Car or Bus excursions tend not to be promotive of the
written word but, if by fore-thought he should have taken
along a small tape recorder, the Excursionist can transcribe
his thoughts at a later date. This practise has much to
recommend it.

Air travel, of course, tends to be mind-numbing in the
extreme and can be discounted as a medium for the
conduct of self expression. However, for really serious
thinking, voyages over oceans are second to none other.

Whatever the ambience, however transient the medium, no
matter what subjugable influences abound, the important

thing is to *'get it down on paper'*. Once there it
eschews reliance on mere cranial retention, subject as it
would be to the myriad imperfections of that unhappy
agency, and remains, as long as the parchment exists in a
referential situation, open to inspection by any interested
party either immediately or in years hence.
This is definitely the preferential condition.
Pursue it (if indeed you can understand it. Read it again --
it works.)

The Venturer, by his very nature, will have already sought
for and obtained that enlightenment of spirit that marks
him out from his fellows. He will have laid aside the
Social 'rules' that are put up as safeguards by grave and
imperturbable defenders of the status-quo. These
misguided folk would rather read in a newspaper *'the
journalist's opinion of what he thinks may have happened
on a particular occasion'*, and believe that sentiment,
rather than give it the scant regard it deserves before
moving on to more significant undertakings.

But the Venturer should also be wary. Once this open-
minded state of self-liberation has been achieved, there is a
tendency to want to share it with others.
To do this is to become a Bore.

Look instead for the 'like-minded', with whom a mutual
rumination on such good fortune may be indulged, and
leave it at that. The others will not understand, nor will
they want to. They will remain steadfastly incanting that,

"You can't eat curry for breakfast!" –

- never daring enough, themselves, to try it; and all the while consuming yet another standard breakfast plate of bacon and eggs.
Leave them be. Write down your thoughts for others to read if they will; but it will not be the 'bacon and egg' brigade.

They are happy enough where and how they are - in the 'now' that is their citadel.

ALPHA

Leave want wide and needs still unfulfilled,
Among the paths confining those they guide.
Shake your mantle from the social skilled
And shout aloud the feelings that you hide.

Though others give you mock and turn away,
What little can they know of higher planes,
Where greater values scorn the workaday?
They wish you where conformity constrains.

To few of us are granted eyes that see
Beauty, challenge, in unlikely things.
For most, their best is mediocrity
That, sated, cloys in tuneless murmurings.

Wherever his journeys take him, the Rambler will
have a closer mind-link with other races than that to which
his stay-at-home counterpart could ever aspire.
Tragedies that overtake them are seen by him in a very
different light, and probably 'closer to home' than is
comfortable.
Such an occasion might well be the invasion of a small
European Country by its larger and more aggressive
neighbour; and there have been a few of those, even in our
time.

THE IMPRISONED MIND

Have I the right to write in blood
Thoughts that need no understanding?
But though the State itself contracts
And groups of people are disbanding,
I have the wherewithal to think
And keep my mind and soul expanding.

So, when they start to think aloud
And fill this world with light of years;
And when they start to see inside,
To empty themselves of empty fears;
Then they will stop and start again
And never stop till time is theirs.

Then will I have the right to write
And all mankind will hear my plea;
But now I stop and never start,

As existence exists not for me.

One of the consequences of constant travel is the lack of 'special relationships' that might be found along the way (you know the sort of thing – girl/boy-friends, marriage and the like) and therefore there exists a tendency to examine the validity of such interdependencies.

QUESTING

When legacies, entrusted squarely,
Turn to less than any stone;
When standing honest, guileless, guiltless
Leads to living life alone;
How can you, with all your fancies,
Hope to love? It is not real!
How become enmeshed, entangled
And enslaved by that ordeal?

There does not have to be a real companion nor an expedient occurrence to occasion the Traveller's entry in his Notebook.

Perhaps, after all, he is merely addressing himself through that medium, but with a thought to his alter-ego - that most secret of all our characteristics.

ADVICE

Think back through long, dark, distant years;
Think back to boyhood raptures.
Take back the mind in gentle time;
Find what the memory captures.

The first, fond, frightening wakes of thought,
The good times and the plenty;
The last, long, lingering days of youth,
Until they too were empty.

The road to great and better things,
That treads on expectation,
And then that sudden, longed-for day,
When all became conviction.

The fumbling, often hopeless quest,
That verged on inspiration.
The joining of two outcast hearts
Despite the condemnation.

Think back - think back upon these things;
Think back; don't let them pine,
For in the dullest, dreary days,
Their light will truly shine.

Rudyard Kipling's book ***'The Light that Failed'*** is a particularly poignant account of Travel, Life, Love and Tragedy. In its day it enjoyed great popularity but has sadly fallen out of favour in recent times. Set in the Middle East and in London, it concerns a War Artist whose lot it is to become blind - not suddenly but in a steady decline. It is a moving tale, and it is remembered in the following piece:

ON THE LIGHT THAT FAILED

I remember seeing all the wonders of the little things
That lie forgotten and unnoticed in our lives.
I saw the colours change and live in majesty;
Unseen, yet making sights indelible.
I saw the many dwellings and the homes
Of all the different peoples of the earth
And all the land that stretched away to heaven,
Mountains, forests, plains and seas,
In colours felt and depth beyond despair.

I listened and I heard the sound of worlds
And though I listened hard, I heard no more.
But now I hear those sounds like thunder
Echoing back and forth about my brain.
I see the sounds inside my head
And scream within that prison, "Let me live!

"Let me see again the wonders that I miss!"

For now I only hear - I cannot see,
And all the vision of a brilliant, flashing world
Has gone.....

One of the problems of being *'away'* is that of kit-storage. Inevitably gear must be left behind and, to that end, the Traveller should find some secure stowage for those articles that have particular value to him. Leaving such things with friends is, on the face of it, a good idea; until the burglar selects their house for his next foray. That is when the friend feels so rotten at having to explain that the safeguarded articles have been taken, albeit along with his own.

In this case there were hand-tools from the late 19th and early 20th century that could never be replaced, nor could that wonderful workmanship ever again be copied.
It was particularly sad when three generations had nurtured and used these implements, to think of them, probably rusting and ill-used or even just thrown away; but, more importantly – never again available for use by those who loved them.
It all seemed such a waste.

LOST LINKS TANKA

These were artefacts
My Grandsire loved and guarded.
The thief who took them,
Counting on their worth, also

Stole a little of my soul.

It is at moments like these that anger swells within and sheer rage craves vent. But the Excursionist, if he is nothing else, is at least in control of himself and it is here that he sees another use for his Notebook - that of Father Confessor and Listening Ear.

It is here that he can let his feelings wash away and soothe his agitated brain.

The written word and the action of writing is indeed '... *a balm to ease the mind.'*

THE PASSING

Look down, you swollen clouds above;
Look down and see the ever winding way.
Look down, through black, wind-driven rain;
Look down and see the progress of our day.
Look down, you carrion ghosts of fear;
Look down and learn - before you pass away.
(for)
The end of all things comes in time,
A Passing, often held by men of times with fear;
When all who ever walked this earth
And sang sweet songs and tunes,
Though days were drear,
Shall see again with eyes anew,
And in a different light,
Those treasures they hold dear.

And on that day,
When darkness turns to light,
When all the hidden yearnings of our hearts
Shine forth like lanterns
In a many-facet star of night,
Our secret souls will cry for one to hear,
Who surely rules our fate
And all we dare.

Wherever his journey takes him, the Adventurer should always wear, in his hat, a Red Rose on 23rd April.
In fact, roses being particularly difficult to obtain in desert regions, he should include a silk one among the content of his Ditty Box.

SAINT GEORGE'S DAY TANKA

Revelling over,
Cast down when sought by a bee,
Pollen from the Rose,
Now Rose again, returned with
Old pride stirring her petals.

-o0o-

SONGS

In 1981 the Falkland Islanders had a musical tradition that was second only to the Outer Hebrides. Based on Fiddles, Melodeons and Banjos, with the occasional assistance of a Piano Accordion (from he who could afford to have it shipped-out to the South Atlantic), the tunes that were played at the Gatherings and Sheerings were very Scottish in origin. Indeed one could almost imagine oneself in the Western Isles at a Ceilidh, there was so little difference. Maybe thirty musicians would form the 'Band' and the ensuing 'Jamboree' would make for a superlative 'knees-up'.

In 1986 the Headmaster of the Islands' School reported that not a single child was learning to play a musical instrument. The Musicians themselves seemed to have disappeared (except for **Billy Morrison**, one of the very few piano-accordionists) and the whole community to have sunk into the morass of mediocrity that is video-tapes, personal stereos, computer games and 'boogie-boxes'.
For certain-sure* one casualty of the later part of the 20th century is the ability among ordinary folk to create their own entertainment and the willingness to perform it. This decline has been slowly creeping upon us a little at a time. The reason for the almost instant change in the Falkland Islands was the sudden influx of several thousand Servicemen, from two continents, and the subsequent introduction of easily obtainable electrical entertainment equipment. Ten years later, nothing had altered.

*(that's 'Formula One-speak'; I just thought I would slip it in. BB)

No doubt, much the same thing could be said about the Royal Navy.

There was a time when shipboard entertainment meant sea-shanties and ship's concerts, or *'sod's operas'*, as they were known. (Ship's Onboard Diversion?) Then, talent was found in the most unlikely places and the most improbable people:

a **Leading Stoker** who was a virtuoso on the Spoons;

the **Captain's secretary** who played a mean Jazz Clarinet;

the **Flight-deck Officer** whose Tuba could hold the bass line together;

the **Physical Trainer**; a twelve-string guitarist who also wrote amusing songs;

an **Able Seaman** whose Zither-mandolin provided the treble counterpoint;

a **Chief Air-engineer** with a Mandolaganjal-liaka (a cross between a mandola, a banjo and a balalaika) whose fingering/strumming was paramount;

the **Chief Engine Room Artificer** with a Pogo-stradavarious (a booted broom-stick, carrying a myriad of nailed-on bottle-tops and played with a notched stick);

and, finally, the **Watch-keeping Lieutenant** who wrote and sang the songs, played an eclectic collection of noise-makers (whistles, bells, duck-calls and the like) and who had the largest Kazoo in the world – named 'Hector'.

These were but a small collection of willing performers in an Aircraft-carrier, who entertained their fellow shipmates

at sea and in harbour; and played seventy-six concerts for
the Ship's Company in such unlikely places as:
the Governor of the Bahamas' Grand Summer Ball;
the Casino Square after the Monaco Grand Prix race;
on the postage-stamp-sized flight-deck of a Fleet Oiler in
mid-Atlantic;
the Malta International Folk Festival;
in the depths of the Grand Bazaar of Istanbul;
and finally to an audience of two thousand Sailors and
Royal Marines in mid-ocean on the way back from
America.

They were called by the rather unusual, but memorable
name of *'The Malawi International Airways String
Quartet'*, and for a glorious year and a half held sway as
the ship's fabricator of musical frolics. Come the end of
the commission, however, they all went their separate
ways to other appointments - and never met with each
other again.
Such is the way of the Voyager, the Traveller, the Rover
and the Sailor.
But, such also is the potency of musical appreciation that,
years later, when meeting-up with any of the two thousand
souls who had been onboard at the time, talk immediately
turned to those performances and how much they meant to
the Souls-onboard.
If ever there was a justification for the 'Party Piece', this
surely was it.

Here, below, so that the reader can share in some measure the remarkable *MIASQ* experience, are three of the songs that delighted all those Sailors, Airmen, Royal Marines and Soldiers, in the days before 'boogie-boxes' and personal stereos were everyone's buffer against the world. Not only that but you are most welcome to use them to further your own position in the case of having to *'do a party piece'* at some social gathering.

THE AUTOMOTIVE ALCOHOLIC ROAD-HOG

You've heard them all before in every Pub and Bar,
The man who seems to worship the religion of the Car.
He'll tell you of the journeys that he's made both far and
wide,
The roads he used to get there, he will number them with
pride,
The A 11, B 13 and road-works outside Rhyll
And how he averaged 'thirty' and you guess he always will.

But I'm the Automotive Alcoholic Road-hog.
I've got a car that really beats them all.
I've had the chassis lowered till it sits upon the ground;
Got 'meggas' up my tail-pipe to amplify the sound.
In the middle of the night, I'll drive round and round the
town,
Coz I'm the Automotive Alcoholic Road-hog.

Now, you've heard them all before in every Pub and Bar,
The man who seems to worship the religion of the Car.
You've seen him with his chequered hat and handle-bar
moustache,
Who says he's driven thirty years and never had a
'craash!'
And when you see his car you're not surprised he's still
alive,
For he'll polish it each Sunday and it never leaves his
drive.

But I'm the Automotive Alcoholic Road-hog.
I've got a car that really beats them all.
I've got so many spotlights that my car looks like a toad.
At night, when you are driving, though my circuits
overload,
I'll flash the whole lot at you till you drive right off the
road.
I'm the Automotive Alcoholic Road-hog.

Yes, you've heard them all before in every Pub and Bar,
The man who seems to worship the religion of the Car.
You know the one whose window-stickers prove he's
travelled far,
Who hugs the middle of the road at twenty miles an hour.
You never can get past him, though you hoot and flash and
wave;
His car and he have got one foot and one wheel in the
grave.

But I'm the Automotive Alcoholic Road-hog.
I've got a car that really beats them all.
My 'slipstream-double-torque-converter-aerofoil' is new;
I find, in heavy traffic, when I'm stuck behind that queue,
That the faster that I drive - the smaller gaps I can get
through.
I'm the Automotive Alcoholic Road-hog.

HYPOCONDRIACOSIS

She has a free-fall shoulder and a dislocated knee.
Her clavicle is critical; her sternum's arthritical.
Her scapula's psychotic and her coccyx is thrombotic.
She's addicted to that osteopathy.

She's pulled her sternomastoids and her gluteus maximi.
Her inter-costal triceps have become her quadri-biceps.
Her semitendinosis have destroyed her little toeses.
She's a martyr to her physiotherapy.

She's got TB. She's gone seedy. She's got spas-muscular pain.
Her ulcers are homogenised. Her kidneys have been sterilised;
Foreign objects cut from the tangle of her gut.
Radiography is driving her insane.

She lost her contact lenses while syringing out her ears.
She's lost her sense of smell and deodorant as well.
Her tonsils have revolted and her adenoids have bolted
And her larynx and her voice have disappeared.

Her bunions are the biggest that the world has ever seen.
She has such fallen arches that she counters counter marches.
Her corns are astronomical, her toe-nails anatomical.
She's got verrucas growing on her spleen!

She's had drillings for her fillings; metal caps upon her teeth.
Her inter-dental cavities show dietary depravities.
Supra-molar plaque has 'polly-filled' the cracks
And her incisors are rotting underneath.

Chorus:
But she's my darling. She's my beauty. She's my lady of delight
And I love the bits and pieces that I gather up each night.

(Thanks are due to **'Dickie Barr'** who co-wrote this piece of whimsy – in about a 'stand-easy'.)

THE PIXIE SONG

On Aberley Bank, back of Clows Top and Cloebury,
Not far from the Washing Pool and the Old Martley Road
And hard by the Dark Wood, where rooks keep their
watches,
There's a small bramble bush, the abode of a Toad.

This Toad had a visa stamped into his passport,
A six-month's work-permit to help pay his way;
An immigrant visitor, that was his station;
A Horned Toad who hailed from the U S of A.

Alouishous de-Vere Debonair was his handle.
His skin was as slimy and horny as that
And he lived all alone in his bramble-bush shelter
And he beat up the Fairies with a small cricket bat.

The Fairy Policeman got fed-up and chocker
And as for the Young Fairy Doctor, he found
That the mending of gossamer wings and smashed noses
Was more than his magical powers could confound.

So a letter they wrote on a frost-spangled dew drop
And sent it by Bluebird away 'cross the sea
And they got for themselves a Hired Toad from Texas
Who shot Alouishous for a magical fee.

So if you're a Toad and you live in the brambles

And you knock Fairies off about six times a day,
Then beware of the Toad in the Tall Hat from Texas;
He's been granted asylum, - and the Fairies are gay!

chorus:
Ahrr, ahrr, I'm a little Pixie. Ahrr, ahrr, I skip around all
day.
Ahrr, ahrr, some parsnip wine'll fix 'ee.
It makes me young and frisky when the Fairies are at play.

There are various refinements that may be applied to this
song. The tune for it may be obtained from the British
Library of Folk Dance and Song, or you could make your
own melody; it is 'the words' that are the thing.

When delivering the last half of the last line of the last
verse, it pays to assume the voice and actions of the 'High
Camp' theatrical practitioner. It kind-of 'makes' the punch
line.

When singing in the chorus, *'Ahrr, ahrr, I skip around all
day.'* – it is traditional to do a 'high kick', once again in
best 'high camp' style. But be warned.....

I was performing this song at the Peter Tavy Inn, on
Dartmoor, with the backing of the finest, ceilidh-band in
the West-country – ***'The Muckchuckrz'*** – and made the
'kicks' with no problem. That was until I came to the last
chorus.

Here I put in a higher kick than usual and 'stumphed' my head at full 'lift' straight into an ancient and substantial oak ceiling-beam. Stunned by the impact, I staggered back and fell into the huge fireplace (with burning log-fire) – completely in time with the music; - -
to the riotous applause from the assembled company.

Ah well, anything for the 'crack'!

But probably the best adjunct to the performance of this song was that inserted by that brilliant piano accordionist and song-writer, the late **Geordie Hesplop**. After each chorus, he would repeat the previous verse/chorus, - but in German. Now, Geordie did not speak German but, much in the style of *'Instant Shakespeare'*, knew the rudiments of the language construction and, most importantly, the 'sound' of it. Using these attributes, his rendition of the Chorus would be....

Ahrr, ahrr, Ich bin a kliner Pixiestichikl.
Ahrr, ahrr, Ich rock around the clock - Jock.
Ahrr, ahrr, der parshnipp vinesill fix 'ee.
Ich makes me young unt friskish vhen der Faaries
summat play.

-oOo-

<u>VERSE</u>

It must be said that the songs in the previous chapter are a little on the long side and their tunes are rather obscure. For the Accomplished Musician this should not prove too much of a problem, as a suitable musical delivery can easily be cobbled together; however, for the Rover who has no musical bent, the lack of a tune will, perforce, require the rendition to be of a 'declamation' rather than a 'vocalization'. That's fine. They will do just as well 'said' as 'sung'.
Go to it!

But for those dead set on 'recitation', something at which our Victorian ancestors were dab hands, here is a selection which will hold the attention of the audience and occasion more than a giggle or two.

THE PARTY

It was a party of the poshest kind
With sausage rolls and VP wine
And mushy-looking things on toast,
So small that they were missed by most.

The Host had neither spared expense
Nor expected recompense

And every guest had been presented
With a medallion - newly minted.

Well, nearly all were new as new,
Excepting maybe just a few,
And these were given out the last
To those whose cars were not so fast.

St Christopher, the medal was.
"I'm giving them away because
"I hope my guests will all arrive
"Safe and sound and still alive.

"A new St Chris will do the trick
"And if their car is old and sick,
("As well I know that some there are
"Who can't afford a shiny car,)
"Then second hand will do for them
"And new, unused for richer men."

And so they came, both rich and poor,
From far afield and just next door;
From Wetwang, Ludlow and Devizes
The people came, all different sizes;

Tall and thin or short and fat,
In trousers, frocks, fur coats and spats,
In suits of many different hues,
Some in sandals, some in shoes.

Some even came with nothing on
But they were quickly set upon
(And, painted red and yellow stripes
Like Fire-Chief surcoat prototypes);
Then, ushered on their way rejoicing,
They made for the nearest level-croissing.

The guests kept coming; more and more
Came streaming through that open door
And set upon what was provided
With rapt attention - undivided.

Then, in that wildly eating crowd,
One person stood and shouted loud,
"Look! What is that that's just arrived,
"That pile of fruit and butterflies?"

They looked and saw, as he had cried,
A monstrous heap of fruit outside.
With one accord they all rushed out
And, letting forth a lustful shout,
They ate it down to core and pip
And that annoyed me; gave me gyp.

But worse it was for Auntie Ada –
For they'd eaten the hat that I had made her.

THE BAYONET! THE BAYONET!

It may be that *'The Bloody Gobbets of Flesh'* (see earlier)
is not considered suitable for some gatherings – even in its
attenuated form. Worry not. Here is a substitute that is
over rather more quickly; maybe even before the more
sensitive listener has realised what it is all about.
And what is it all about?

Choice – that's what it is all about.
You can choose to do this one - in place of the other.

Once again, the harsher accents of The Glasgow 'Gorbals'
will do better justice to the piece than 'The Morningside';
unless of course you wish to really soften the impact; in
which case you could always go way out on a limb and try
the 'Perceived BBC' accent.
It would be a risk, sure; but it all depends on how
confident (or drunk) you are.
Give it a go, anyhow.

Write and let me know how you get on.

I stuck my bayonet in him an' I shuggled it about.
First his spleen and gall bladder, then his bowels fell out.
I put my hand into his chest an' ripped his lungs apart
An' cut his liver from him, an' then tore out his heart.

This bloody chunk, still beating, I lifted in my hand
An' threw it down upon the rocks an' on it took my stand.
Each ear I partly severed and pulled out by the roots
An' sucked his eyes out one by one an' spat 'em in his
boots.
I crushed his neck and vertebra an' hacked at it as well
An' threw his body in the swamp........
I never knew him well.

IF I WAS GOOD

We all learned the poem *'If'*, by **Rudyard Kipling** when we were at school, and very high-sounding and apposite advice it is too; in fact, incredibly difficult to live up to – although we do our best.

This recitation exists on a lower plane that that and is more of an observational question than a recipe for living. However, it does have its merits and, although I doubt it will achieve the fame of **RK**'s original, it does deserve an airing.

As the famed Entertainer – **'Jethro'** - would say, *"Go you ahead!"*

If I was very, very good
And brushed my teeth and ate my food,
Cleaned my shoes and stood up straight,
Went to school, was never late;

And if I never answered back
But always and with perfect tact
Told the truth to all who'd hear,
Kept off spirits, wines and beer;

And if I turned the other cheek,
Was always humble, ever meek;
And if I worked so very hard
And never counted on reward;

And if I loved my fellow man,
Despite his faults, as best I can;
Pray, do you think that in the end
I would be better off, my friend?

Or

If I turned out really bad,
A wicked, evil, nasty cad;
Scuffed my shoes and kicked the dog
And picked my nose and swore at God;

If I played truant, never learned
And shouted words that scornf'ly burned;
If I told lies, the blackest kind,
Got plastered out my tiny mind;

And If I stabbed you in the back
And always thought who to attack;
And if I thrived on graft and theft,
Left all relations poor, bereft;

If I distrusted every man
And used his faults to aid my plan;
How can you say I'd surely fall?
How could I? I would own it ALL!

- Wouldn't I?

SAMANTHA

Ah, love – true love! Was it not always the way?
Do you know, the majority of our modern 'folk' songs –
more readily known today as 'pop-songs' – are about the
trials and tribulations of love.
One would have thought that, with such an extensive
canon of the genre, they would have got it right by now.
[But, then again, much the same thing could be said about the scoring of goals in
the plethora of football matches that seem to abound almost every week-end. They
all get so excited!]

Well, here's something just a little different.

Do you remember the lamp-post, Samantha,
Where we stopped on the way to the church?
And do you remember the old wicket gate,
The wattle of willow and birch?

Do you remember the pink apple blossom
That sheltered us once from the rain?
Oh, tell me, Samantha, you haven't forgotten.
Tell me you'll find them again.

Yes, tell me, Samantha, that deep in your heart
You remember the route that we took
Past the church with the bomb-blasted windows
To the rough, wooden bridge o'er the brook;

For tonight the wind blows and the rain lashes down

As we sit by the fire, safe at home.
So I hope you remember the way, little dog,
For tonight you go 'walkies' alone.

BREEKH-TROKHIT AN' THE LAGGART SLOOR

All around the world, in more places than one would care to imagine, Scots and (far worse) Pseudo-Scots insist on celebrating Burns Night. Everyone is kilted-up to the eyebrows; huge amounts of whiskey are consumed; the Haggis is ritually slaughtered and Pipers, who should by rights be playing upon a distant mountain top, march around the table making the deafened air hideous with their droning-baloo. Their instrument is not called the 'doodlesac' by the Germanic race without good reason. It has been said that the definition of a Gentleman is *'.... one who is able to play the bagpipes - but refrains from doing so.'*

That aside, the Pipes are fabulous for rallying soldiers on the Field of Battle (playing *'Black Bonnet'* while storming a heavily defended bridge, for example) or as a spectacle during a 'March through the Town'; and, certainly, every ship should have at least one Piper.

[**Geordie Heslop** was once asked, when hearing a distant piper in a Scottish forest, *"Geordie, are those War-pipes?"* To which he replied, *"No, they're his!"*]

But do not play, please, in the confines of a dining-room where the drone-pipes barely clear the ceiling and the bulk of the Piper has difficulty circumnavigating the table in the first place. However, as it is all part of the Burns Night *'tarteeb'**, I suppose it must be endured.

*'tarteeb': an Arabic word that has no simple equivalent in English but which means '.... the whole rigmarole .... what it is all about.'

Another important ritual of the evening is the recital of
poetry from the Great Man; or, as the Scot would say,
simply, "... *from Himself.*"
Very few people understand what is being said but none
will admit it. Ask a Scot what it all means and he will say,
"Aye, that's for me to know and you to find out."
A direct translation would be, *"No idea, mate!"*

For the Adventurer attending a Burns Night, it is essential
to be armed with a piece of poetry to do justice to the
evening; and here it is.

By fallow Creakht an' sparklin' dew
Yon years flit storrikly awa'.
It little fashes us the noo'
When half our Tummatours gang gra'.
Five noo' an' twunty be the score
That twice the Limmer Mon hath passed,
For what may mak' a mon sae dour
As meetin' wi' his Cragorast?
Beware the Wimpril-Lassie, Mon!
Keep yer Breekhters twixt yer knees;
Or else the Feemell-Trokht will come
An' fairly give yer Loure a Squeeze!

Aye, awa' the Wimpril-Lass
That laggarts wi' an Ochtodair;
Freel an' frookhit be the Sloor
Who looks a-preekin' mair an' mair.
O yer Pelter Sorranokh,

See the serraf Martabie;
Kind indeed the Breekhter's Loure
That hides itself beside yer knee.
So, wi' fufty Feemell-Trokhts,
All set aboot wi' gammerstaires,
Shall the Wimpril-Lassie come
To squeeze yer Loure instead o' her's.

Sadly play yon Brokhit Pipes
'N softly toll yer bell;
Ah, sloors the serraf Martabie,
The Breekhter's Loure comes fell.
Naiver noo' the Wimpril-Lass
All freel an' frookhit stands
For awa' the Limmer Mon,
A-preekin', flits these lands.
Lost yer Pelter Sorranokh
An' dread yer gammerstaires,
Dour yer storrik Feemel-Trokhts
That squeeze yer Loure an' Her's.
Now no need o' Tummatours,
No Laggart's pantomimes,
For yon's the road that fashes us to strangled paradigms.

Of course, you will have recognised this as Burns – Nobby
Burns – which you will have remembered from the end of
the *'After Dinner Speech'*; but there is absolutely no need
to tell that to anyone else.

In past times, when this piece of whimsy has been employed to grace the occasion, it has been noticed that the 'aficionados' nodded sagely, took another dram and mumbled,

"Aye, Burns. Marvellous poetry."

...and it never seemed necessary to disillusion them.

Similarly, being a Fiddler and invited to perform for a Burns Night by the Caledonian Society, it was not deemed necessary to mention that all the music that had been played was actually Irish.
After all, no-one had noticed and everyone had had a splendid time

Note: Have another look at the piece above, discard the 'odd' words and phrases, they are only decoration, and see if you can fathom out what it is all about; because it does make sense.

SHOLTOS AT QUEBEC

Here is another offering from the 'Die-hards' own poet-in-resonance, Oropesa Molgoggah-Fid-Sholto. It explains why the ceremonial cloak, that each officer sports, is shorter than the usual and is ragged about the edges.
This 'cameo' gives insight to a small but important aspect of General Wolfe's assault on Quebec in 1757. We all learned at School about the stealthy approach made by boats *'.... with muffled oars'*; but no-one ever explained how they were muffled nor who muffled them.
Perhaps, now, all that will be seen to be on account of the ***'Sinbads'*** who, because their balloons were 'grounded' due to a lack of combustibles, had nothing much else to do at the time anyway.

Loud were the cannon in the rolling battle's roar.
High rose the neighing of the horses on the shore.
Dread were the curses that the facing armies swore.
Soft rolled the vapours of the acrid fires of war.
Heavy was the burden that the gallant soldier bore;
Halberdiers from Barradoune and Seypoys from Jahore.
Soiled flew the pennants from the lances, red with gore.
Busy was the clacking of the signal semaphore.

Cunningly exulted stood the Naval Commodore.
Secret was the progress as the cutters pulled inshore.
Solidly advancing were the ones who went before.

Silent were the ripples of the Sholto-muffled oar,
Made from ration boxes nailed to bits of two-by-four.
Ragged hung the mantles, from where each strip was tore.
Down fell the City when the 'Die-hards' stepped ashore.
When the siege was ended, quoth the Sinbads,
"Nevermore!"

-oOo-

PUZZLES

The Reader will, by now, have a pretty good idea of how the Expat survives his self imposed exile and what measures he may take to deal with any problems that it engenders. Hopefully he will also have equipped himself, the Reader – that is, with enough extracts from this book to stuff in his Ditty Box against the day when he himself encounters those enumerated here.

There remains, therefore, only one thing more – to enliven his own mind. For that reason the following conundra* are included.

They, all of them, have something to say.

See if you can discover what/why it is.

* It should be *'conundrums'*- but that sounds rather clumsy; *'conundra'* is so much better.

BELOW LONDON

Free verse in a subway station
Clicking the ticket machines;
Coats pushed forward to anoraks,
High heels cracking the tiles;
Posters watching with silent eyes
The steps climbing up - clacking.

Hot, wet breath rushing through the dark,
Clutching at a suitcase;
Music toiling in the twilight
Lost, catching in the hair;
Concrete vibrating like black steel
While shadows are crouching.

IN HOPE

Sorrowfully reason's gleaming,
Tainted by impurity of thought,
Reconciles in lust filled minds
And is enclosed by fetters of despair.

Now, within that visited abyss,
Generations sit, whose bright
Exchange doth virtue iterate.

Thus, with frequency increasing,
Immersed, devoid of rancour's ill,
Merit shall with changes in its thrall,
Even with Hibernian Rhetoric,
So in temporal sphere become unusual.

(A clue: two elderly, dour Scots farmers discussing affairs at a ceilidh, as seen in the film *'Local Hero'*. Look for the last line.)

EASY STREET

If recognition was the prize
For those whose faults in others' eyes
Were masked with envy, I surmise
That such a feeling cultivated,
Leaving one but semi-hated,
Would mark the path that glorifies
The mediocre compromise.

CALL THE HANDS

And so, with slow abiding haste,
These Ships, small cockleshells of fate,
Wend a wandering, watery way
Towards the bulk of fitful shores.
Can we now see the sleeping Watch,
That holds the never ending cycle of its time?
For now, amid the rays of growing sun,
Hoisted in the brilliant sphere of heaven's orb,
Morning, like a blanket to our minds,
Rises here and on the distant shore.

(Let us say that this is *'rather Shakespearean'* in its instant form and that the clue is in the Title.)

THE MONOLINGUAL GOAT

(An 'Enhanced Tanka')

Arabian Goats
Are not bilingual, yet we
Greet them in English;
We persist, conscious of their
Monolinguality;
So perhaps we are
Only talking to ourselves.

IDIOTS' LANTERNS

(An 'Enhanced Tanka')

Malevolently
They brood over living-rooms,
Open prisons all,
Whose inmates, unknowingly
Suborned to witlessness , stare,
Mediocrity entranced,
Deep into their Nemesis.

TEA TANKA

From these two beakers
Breakfasting and Teas are drunk
In strict rotation.
They are stranger-duplicates
Who stalk each other's settlings.

And, finally, in this chapter, an Epic Poem that won the Prize, from a reputable Poetry Society, for the Best Poem of the Season, way back in the Seventies. I wonder how it will fare in today's rarefied atmosphere of *'the Internet'*. Apropos of which; there is an old saying that concerns an unlimited supply of monkeys, an equal number of typewriters, an ultimate length of time and the works of Shakespeare. The invention of the first tends to disprove the efficacy of the second.

THE GORGON AND THE EGG

And as I looked above the trees
Without a single over-sliding fear,
I noticed, and with such relief bethought,
That all of Nature's creatures,
Whether sensible or fat,
And only in their passing gone before us,
Had put aside their one important eye
And lost forever in their way
That last, fond cherished matter of the world.

And though the greatest being of them all
Had never thought to leave the Armitage,
Still shall the trumpet sound and, egg-like, waddle on
Towards the Foe, whose gnashing limbs,
Clutched with spears of doubt
And scimitars of disbelief,

Are spread in endless symmetry,
The last expression to relieve.

Oh, never let the Phalanx fail
And leave the broken Shard;
For there, amid the Gloomy Plants,
Their poison breath but a reminder of ourselves,
Lies the ever thickening circle
Where, and stood between the Monoliths,
A Gorgon, with its soulful helpers, waits
Amid the weeds of darkness and despair;
Awaits in splendour and the depths of time,
Replete with half-digested lies of martyrdom.

And though half thought of in her way
As outwardly removed from others' hope,
She waits with all the cunning of her kind,
As though bereft of any mental fire
And cut, cut through - beyond the bones of truth
And love - to such a lost regime as only can be found
Beside the Egg.

And so shall all who venture forth,
Believing in their own remaining traits,
Reveal themselves as true and useless fools
To those whose armour joints are stained
And clogged with poison and remorse.

Look not away beyond the stars,
Where all shall one day end their time,

For though a brandished pillar of the world
Be fallen in the emptiness and,
In its haste is set afire in flight,
So shall those precious seeking-men,
Despite their safest lanterns of deceit,
Lie with their fellows in the wastes of time,
Their breathing like the pools of nothing
In the Central Hall that none has seen.
So shall it end for all who dare
The Gorgon and the Egg.

STRANGE RECIPES

Up to now, the traveller has been largely concerned with
the written and spoken word to gain favour with his hosts
and to achieve the higher plain of facilities on offer to a
favoured guest. However, there is a further way that these
might be forthcoming and that is from the ever popular
medium of 'cooking'.
Turn out a palatable dish – or, even better, something
totally new – and his place in the hospitality stakes is
assured. Once again, it could be the difference between the
pull-out bed in the box-room and the more promising,
*"Do use the spare room as your temporary home. We are
having a bit of a house party at the week-end but no-one
will disturb you there."*

But it is not only for that satisfying outcome that this part
of the book is added. Oh no! There is a more important
aspect – that of the welfare of the voyager himself (or
herself – if indeed such a distinction is deemed necessarily
to be made. There! I have made it now; so, let that suffice.)
'Cooking', as seen in television programmes, in an ever
proliferating spiral, is all very well for the sedentary,
home-staying aficionado but of little practical use to the
Wanderer. Most of the time, he has little access to the
plethora of utensils and gadgets available to that particular
character. In reality (and this is not a 'show') he must
make do with what he has around him – particularly if
voyaging in a sea-craft where fuel, water and rations are at
a premium. Any man who is capable of turning out

interesting and nourishing victuals in such an environment will be doubly welcomed wherever he may end up.

What follows here is the result of over half a centaury's experience – from Student Days to Elder Times; from Middle Eastern sojourns to ancient recipes garnered from a long departed generation. Experience is the key and the following collection leans heavily (as will become apparent) upon it. There may be one or two anomalies, but, bear with it and all will become clear.

<u>HISTORICAL GEMS FROM THE ROYAL NAVY</u>

Back in the mid 1970s, the then Commander in Chief Fleet sent a signal to his ships, saying,

"You are to have more fun!"

The 'Navy-that-Was' looked at itself and murmured,

"Well, that's put the kibosh on that! Shame, really; we were quite enjoying ourselves."

For the 70s were the last knockings of: many ships, 'cheap commands', foreign squadrons, much 'fun' and interesting deployments. Now, all that has gone. There are fewer ships around [just recently they scrapped our Fleet Flag-ship – which was not even twenty years old - 2017], more work for reduced numbers, cuts, cuts and more cuts – yet still the same tasks to be done, just less equipment with which to do it and less time in which to achieve each end. Poor dears; there cannot be much fun left in a 21st century Navy.

There is not much we can do about it, but perhaps the following 'dits' will achieve some smiles of nostalgia and a warm glow in which to bask with a might-have-been. So, let's see what the 'ditty bag' holds; ah-ha – a recipe book belonging to ancient mariners; who invite all to share in dreams of long ago.

167

The first one

'KAI'

Description

This is '*a cup of cocoa*' as you have never known it.
I first tasted it when, aged five, I was on a camping trip in
Glen Coe with my father. Early one morning I was
awakened to view the Morning Star and the 'first cloud'.
This last appeared out of a clear, crepuscular, blue sky as a
small puff of smoke all on its own. Within fifteen minutes
it had been joined by a whole host of other clouds and the
day had begun. What happened to the weather after that is
not recorded but it was probably a mixture of sun, wind,
rain and, of course, the fabled and infinitely irritating
Scottish 'Knadge'. [This is a cross between a 'Knat' and a 'Midge' and has
the ability to wriggle through mosquito netting just to get at you in the middle of
the night.]
Anyway, to return to the Kai. The lad was presented with
his mug of the stuff by the Able Seaman who was
accompanying the party as camp attendant. Whether it
actually had a small tot of rum in it or not is left to your
imagination; however, the occasion was memorable
enough to be transferred here many, many years after it
occurred. I have been hooked on the stuff ever since.

Note: you will notice that the word 'pusser' occurs
regularly. It is the soubriquet commonly used by sailors to
describe all things Naval.

Ingredients

-A Pusser's chocolate block – well, more of a brick, really.
-Some sugar of the granulated variety.
-Several tins of condensed milk (see note).
-A quantity of water.

Note: you may use evaporated milk if you like but the quantity of sugar will have to be adjusted to suit. It is not possible to be exact in the quantities of ingredients required as the whole idea of making Kai is just that – an idea. Some can make it and some cannot. Those who can – guard their secrets; those who cannot – have nothing to say on the matter.

What you may need

-A steam-powered Warship. Well, good luck in finding one of them these days!
-A large, aluminium mess-deck 'fanny' (a cross between a saucepan and a bucket – although, be warned, modern health and safety requirements advise against using aluminium utensils. It is up to you, really; do you want the authentic Pusser's Kai experience or do you want to survive?).
-A Pusser's dirk (that's a kind of heavy duty clasp-knife, with a spike) or a 'woodsman's knife' from a Pusser's rigging-set. Make sure it is sharp as sharp, though; to set about a task with a blunt knife is as valid as using a pencil to slice chorizo.

-Something with which to stir the whole lot [correct English]. Stick with the aluminium theme and use a Pusser's soup ladle; it will come in useful later for dishing out the brew.

Method

-Obtain from any available corner (perhaps from the 'internet' – as everyone seems to do these days) a block of 'Pusser's Cocoa Chocolate'. It is no good asking anyone in the RN to help; Pusser got rid of the stuff decades ago; and, anyway, the modern, high-tec 'matelot' (as RN sailors still call themselves*) has never heard of 'Kai'.

* **Interesting historical note**: they also used to refer to their ilk as belonging to '*Her Majesty's Royal Corps of Naval Survivors*'.

-Shave a goodly portion of this into a 'mess-deck fanny' with your 'Pusser's Dirk' and add a certain amount of sugar and the contents of some tins of condensed milk.
-Fill to about three quarters the way up with ordinary water (or 'Pusser's water' if you can get it).
-Now, carrying your fanny in your left hand (and remember: '*One hand for the kai, one hand for the ship.*' - it's an old nautical saying), hie-thee to the Engineering spaces of your steam-powered Pusser's warship – assuming that you have found one that works.
-Seek out the Chief of the Engine-room or the Petty Officer Stoker in the Boiler-room and ask if you may have the use of a steam-drain and some of his steam to heat the concoction.
Now, be careful here!

-Test the indicated piece of equipment first by cracking it open a tad to ensure that steam emits. Having tested to see that this really is the steam-drain and not a 'fofo' discharge**, put the pipe into the fanny and then turn on the tap. The steam that emits will boil up the beverage in much the same way that an espresso machine heats milk – but far more quickly and efficiently due to the several thousand units of Pusser's steam-horsepower on the other end of the pipe.

-Once this heating phase is completed, thread a number of cups onto a bent piece of wire and do the rounds of Bridge, Look-outs, Wheel-house, Tiller-flat, Sea-boat Crew and Life-buoy Ghost; all of which watch-keepers will think you are a jolly good fellow and may give you 'sippers' of their 'Tot' in the mess later.

** *'Fofo'* – acronym (or not) for Furnace Fuel Oil – an all pervasive, treacle-like substance that has to be heated before it can be sprayed into the boilers to make the steam with which to heat it in the first place. Wonderful are the ways of Pusser.

Statement. There is no cup of coffee in the world, no matter how well made, that can compare to the efficacy of a good mug of 'Pusser's Kai' for rejuvenating a jaded middle-watch-keeper and quickening interest in the matters of the moment. So, go to it!

Where it can all go wrong

If you do not check that the drain pipe actually does emit steam; if you just shove the pipe into the Kai and turn on the tap; you may find that you have been directed to a vacuum pipe instead and, as soon as you turn on the tap, all your carefully prepared mixture will be sucked out of the fanny by several thousand units of Pusser's steam-horsepower-in-reverse in no seconds flat. [Interestingly, measured in *'inches-of-mercury'*.] This is considered to be a 'jolly jape' by the engineering staff - but your only recourse is to find a place to hide for the rest of the Watch, away from your fellows who are wondering *'...where their **** Kai is!'* And that is a recipe for disaster.

(This happened to Bernie in HMS *Tenby,* but he did survive.)

-o0o-

The second one

PUSSER'S LIMERS

Description

Pusser's Limejuice, or *'Limers'* as it was more readily called, was issued to the Ship's Company of a Royal Navy Ship serving in any potentially sweltering part of the world. Its main ingredients (lime essence and sugar) were supplied in powdered, crystalline form (in sacks) and were mixed up with water in a dustbin that had been specially designated to that purpose.

Ingredients

-A sack of Pusser's Lime Crystals
-A large quantity of Pusser's sugar
-Pusser's water or its equivalent

What you may also need

-A large, galvanized metal dustbin. This should be used only for making 'Limers'. Do not bother to clean it; the 'Limers' will make a much better job of doing that all by itself.
-A wooden spatula that resembles a shaved and flattened base-ball-bat and is used for stirring.
-The use of a 'cold room' for three quarters of a day.

-A Bakelite ladle. It is doubtful that an aluminium ladle would last the distance. (Legend has it that Bakelite was invented by an ex-matelot-chef after he had run out of aluminium serving ladles on his 'permanent loan' allowance.)

-The assistance of two Field Gunners, preferably 'Heavy-end'*.

* *'Heavy end'* – large and extremely muscular Field Gunners who were used to lift the breech-end of the gun when shifting the whole *'equipe'* through, over, round and about the obstacle course that comprised this, the world's toughest 'sport' – that was and is no more. A shame, really, as the Field Gun Run was one of the 'Greats' in National Heritage and a great favourite with the public at the Earl's Court annual Royal Tournament – where it was always the opening exhibit – but which is itself also no more.

Method

-Place the ingredients into the dustbin and add water to about the ¾ mark. If there is no mark – make one. Ask the Chief of the Galley just what quantity of the ingredients to use.

He will tell you – **once**.

Don't ask again.

-Summoning the two Field Gunners, ask them politely to lift the dustbin onto the galley range. They will grunt a bit; don't worry – it is what passes for speech among their genre.

-Bring the content to the boil.

-Once it has bubbled away for an hour or so (stir it every so often with the wooden spatula), have the Field Gunners come back to take the dustbin off the range. Cover it with the dustbin lid and leave to cool.

Later:
Muster the Field Gunners again (this is gonna cost you a 'tot'!) and have them move the bin to be shut away in the Cold Room for the rest of the day, and half the next forenoon.
Here it will quietly brood in the dark.

A long time later:
Come 'Stand-easy' ('Eleven-ziz', as the civilian population has it) the following day, drag the bin to the Galley door in time for 'Limers Issue'. Allow a maximum of one pint per man.

Those too young to draw their 'Tot' (of Rum – yes, I know it was a long time ago but surely you have heard of it) did have the bonus of accepting in its place a small, paper bag of the magic crystals. Have these ready to distribute to the children.

Historical note
Actually drinking Pusser's Limers was an experience in itself. The first draught would bring about the involuntary but violent puckering of the lips and a sharp intake of breath. The remainder would merely cause one to feel that

the enamel was being stripped from the teeth and that fillings were in the process of dissolving.

It really was 'good stuff', particularly when considering.....

What to do next

The 'Issue' having taken place, the remaining 'limers' should be given into the care of the Mate of the Upper Deck, whose Buffer's Party will use it to scrub down the decks.

Another Historical Note

The application of this substance, when mixed with Pusser's Hard Brown Soap (this was in the days when each man would draw a monthly allowance for dhobiing [washing clothes], bathing, shaving etc), brought up a teak deck to a quite brilliant white; although it also tended to 'eat' the soap.

Third Historical Note

'Limers', Pusser's Hard Brown Soap, 'Kai' (amazingly thick and nutritious 'cocoa' guaranteed to wake-up a drowsy Middle-watchman [see recipe above]), Rum, hammocks, 'issue' Passion-killers (cellular underpants [see *'the Gunner'* Tug Wilson – a 'heavy-end' Field Gunner]), sea-boots, oilskins, white Coastal Forces' sweaters, 'herrings-in' (-in tomato sauce, -in a tin, -into you) and Montague Whalers (see Roy Palmer's *'Boxing the Compass – the Oxford Book of Sea Songs'*, page 312-313; *'Songs and*

Ditties of the Fleet' [Barr & Bruen] page 11-15 and Shep Woolley's Album *'Goodbye Sailor'*) all disappeared at about the same time; along with the introduction of plastic Inglefield Clips (which have an alarming failure rate of the type the old, brass ones did not), fibreglass boats and the 'woolly-pulley' (considerably less wind-proof than the good-old battledress top that it had no business replacing - and it has no pockets!).

And some people would have it said that we have advanced!

-oOo-

The third one

MIDSHIPMAN'S OMLETTE

Description

This is a recipe from 1970, so you will have to be diligent in finding the necessary ingredients. It is not even certain that they are available (as most things are supposed to be) on the Internet. However, with the genuine component parts, this should make for a 'memorable feast' (see *'Chiggers in my Tea'* – also by Bernie Bruen).

Ingredients

-A Midshipman.
-Two eggs.
-A Coniston-class Minesweeper.
-A cook/chef.
-Three members of the ship's company.
-A Navigating Officer (NO).
-An Executive Officer (XO) and
-A Captain.

What you will also need

-The connivance of the cook, the ship's company, the navigator and the First Lieutenant (XO) – but <u>NOT</u> the Captain.

Preparation

Note: some planning is required here but as you have little else to do, there should not be a problem.

-Take one of the eggs and hard-boil it (you may get the chef to do this – after all, it is his job). The other egg should remain 'au natural'.
-Once the hard-boiled egg is cool, immerse it in a jar of clear vinegar to soak for two days.
-Remove the egg and allow it to dry.

Method

-Place the Coniston-class Minesweeper on passage from one point in the Middle East to another.
-Choose the time of 'half-an-hour-before-four-o'clock-in-the-afternoon' when the ship is working 'tropical routine'. (This will keep bystanders to a minimum as they will all be asleep down below.)
-Put the Midshipman on the Bridge as 'Officer of the Watch', along with the helmsman, the bos'n's mate and a lookout.
-Make sure that the rubberised deck covering is clean and tidy.
-Gather together in the Chart-room, below the Bridge, the cook (with the eggs), the NO and the XO; but leave the Captain asleep in his cabin.

Now act out the following script:

Midshipman (pissed with power), *"Steady as she goes, helmsman."*

Helmsman, *"Aye aye, sir. Steady as she goes."*

Chef, calling from the Chart-room, *"Permission to come on the Bridge, sir?"*

Midshipman, *"Yes please, chef. What can we do for you today?"*

Chef, entering from below, *"Well, sir, I just wanted to show you this."*

Midshipman, *"What's that, chef?"*

Chef, *"I was in the galley preparing the boys' tea, when I dropped this egg – and it bounced! Look."*

He drops the egg onto the deck, it bounces and he catches it.

Midshipman, with amazement, *"That's incredible. Do it again."*

The chef bounces the egg again and catches it.

Midshipman, *"And that's an ordinary egg? Let me see."*

With sleight of hand, the chef gives to the Midshipman the other egg, who examines it, and hands it back.

Midshipman to bos'n's mate, *"Go and get the Navigator. He's got to see this."*

The bos'n's mate goes below and returns shortly after with the Navigating Officer in tow.

Navigator, *"What's all this, Mid? What's the problem?"*

Midshipman, *"No problem, sir; but the chef dropped an egg in the galley..."*

Navigator, *"So? Get him to clean it up. Why are you telling me?"*

Midshipman, *"No, you don't understand, sir. It bounced."*

Navigator, *"It bounced? What was it – hard boiled?"*
Midshipman, *"No, sir. I've checked it out and it is an ordinary egg. Show him, chef."*
The chef bounces and catches the egg.
Navigator, *"Get the First Lieutenant up. He's the victualler and it's his egg."*
The First Lieutenant comes to the Bridge, where a similar dialogue and demonstration is performed.
Midshipman, to XO, *"Should I get the Captain up, sir?"*
XO, *"Well, I should think he'll want to see this, don't you?"*
Midshipman calls into voice-pipe, *"Captain, sir; Officer of the watch."*
Captain, sleepily, from his cabin, *"Captain...."*
Midshipman, *"Could you come to the Bridge please, Sir?"*
Captain, *"On my way."*
There is a pause while everyone waits for the Captain to traverse three sections and come up three decks from his cabin to the Bridge.
By this time the Midshipman has taken charge of the egg; but, unbeknown to him, it is the fresh egg.
Captain climbs onto the Bridge, *"Yes, Mid. What is it?"*
Midshipman, *"Captain, sir; look at this."*
Midshipman throws the egg onto the deck where it smashes open.
There is a stunned silence.
Captain, *"Your leave is stopped for three weeks – and you can eat that egg!"*

The chef scrapes up the egg, takes it back to the galley and, later, brings up to the Midshipman an omelette – which the Mid then consumes.

(Note: it took the Midshipman forty five years to realise the intricacies of this particular scam.)

-oOo-

The fourth one

'BOMB' SURPRISE

Description

In olden times, back in the 70s, the Naval Base at Portland on the Dorset coast was used to 'work-up' the ships of the Royal Navy, under the direction of Flag Officer Sea Training, or 'FOST' – as he was more popularly known. Particular emphasis was given to anti-submarine warfare and its practices. To this end, a small squadron of Type Fourteen Frigates was used to teach that art to Torpedo and Anti-submarine ratings' classes, operations-room crews and the designated-Captains of similar A/S ships. These Frigates worked hard and long in pursuit of this goal and the Officers of their wardrooms played hard in consequence.

This recipe is a postprandial accomplishment and, although not strictly edible, is quite 'delicious'.

Ingredients

-A formal mess-dinner.
-A quantity of energetic, young officers (one of whom may later attain the rank of Admiral of the Fleet and elevated to the House of Peers– true!)
-A large quantity of sherry - before dinner.
-Wine (red and white) - during dinner.

-Vintage port (go round at least three times) and a good brandy - after dinner.
-A selection of robust Mess-games to enliven the latter part of the evening.
-A spirit of adventure.

What you will also need

-A substantial, helicopter-carrying, 'Six Inch' (gun) Cruiser, commanded by a very senior Captain, in harbour on a Work-up at the time.
-A large roll of Pusser's black masking-tape. [Rather better than the Duct-tape available today – the Navy's 'cure-all' for any and all improvisational tasks.]
-A slalom-kayak and associated gear.
-The conviction that what you are doing is totally valid.

Method

-Assemble for the Dinner in formal attire and enjoy it while you may.
-Imbibe the quantity of alcohol specified.
-After indulging in the Mess-games (including the one that requires you to exit the wardroom via the scuttle (porthole), scale the hull to the upper deck, traverse and descend to the bathroom scuttle on the other side, pass through this and return to the wardroom – all against the clock), someone should exclaim (sotto voce),
"I've got a good idea. Why doesn't … (specify a person) … get in his canoe and 'attack' the Cruiser? You could write 'Fuck-off FOST' in masking tape down the side."

It is likely that this suggestion will be met with universal acclaim by the assembled company.
(**Note**: once this approbation is achieved, there is no room for backing out.)

-Without bothering to change out of formal evening-wear, enter the canoe with a large roll of Pusser's masking-tape on your arm. Paddle under the beams of the jetty and out into the intervening strip of water to approach the Cruiser.

Warning! Warning! Danger! Danger!
The Cruiser, being on 'work-up', will be at a high state of 'alert' against possible attack from swimmers and other nefarious ne'er-do-wells. Consequently you must take care not to be seen.

-To this end, alter course to pass clear of the basin (you probably nearly got run down by a couple of high speed guard-launches anyway, for it is a very dark night and they were not able to see you) and make your way through the jetty-beams until you are alongside the Cruiser's stern, under the jetty, watching people passing to and fro across the gangway above.
-Now make your way up to the bow, pass round it and proceed down the seaward side to about a-midships.
-Stand up in your canoe (difficult one, this, but the alcoholic impetus should aid you) and attempt to 'write' the required message along the side in strips of the masking-tape.

Where it all starts to go wrong - and what to do about it.

-As the ship has probably been at sea recently, it is likely
that there will be a sheen of salt-spray on the paintwork
which will prevent the masking-tape from adhering. If this
is the case, do not worry; merely shift to Plan B.

(**Note**: in enterprises of this sort – always have a Plan B.)

Plan B:
-Shift to the stern of the cruiser and, using convenient ring-
bolts set there, and being sheltered by the flight-deck
overhang (well, look at it on the *internet* under *'RN Cruiser C99 –
images'*), wipe away the salt residue with your shirt.
-Now stick long strips of masking-tape across the ship's
Number (C99) on the sloping transom.
-Once this is completed, return by the same route to your
ship and, basking in the admiration of your fellow officers,
and have another brandy.
Then, your evening complete, retire to bed because there is
an early start next day.

Historical notes

1. When the Type Fourteen Frigate set sail the next
morning, the Cruiser was taken a little by surprise and
rushed to hoist the 'night Ensign', as protocol required.
Both the Officer of the Watch and the Quartermaster were
engaged in doing this as speedily as possible – one on each

half of the flag halyard. The Officer won and the ensign was hoisted upside-down!

2. An ensign hoisted upside-down is an internationally recognised distress signal. Plain to see was the 'limpet mine' attached to the stern, as represented by the masking-tape crossing-out the ship's number. Distressful indeed!

3. Flag Officer Sea Training, the Admiral in charge of the Base, was not best pleased.

4. Ironically the officer responsible for this prank was appointed to the same Cruiser a year later.

He kept very quiet about the incident.

-oOo-

The fifth one

CROMARTY/BURGHEAD LIFEBOAT SANDWICH

Description

This delicacy came about in 1971 due to a chance encounter between the Cromarty Lifeboat and the Moray Outward-bound Sea School.
It takes as its basis the fact that, when preparing for a trip into the mountains and some strenuous mountaineering or rock climbing, the sandwiches that are made for lunch will invariably meld together into one solid lump when jostled around in a rucksack.
From this came the idea that it would save a great deal of effort to make it that way in the first place, as it all goes down the same way in the end.

Ingredients

-Three large slices of bread.
-Lurpak butter in spreadable form. If it is too cold – sit on it for a bit before unwrapping.
-Ham or Spam or other prepared-meat substance/substitute.
-Any one (or more) of Shiphams potted meat or fish spreads [if you want to be really daring – Bloater].
-A banana.
-Branston pickle.
-Honey.

-Any kind of jam.
-Sandwich spread.
-Mustard.
-Bovril

Interesting 'lifestyle' note:
Bovril is a meat extract; Marmite is a yeast extract.
It is said of Marmite that you either love it or hate it. This statement has no relevance. The simple truth is:
Bovril is for Boys; Marmite is for Girls – in much the same way as that proper Boys (who have not been 'got at' by their mothers) tie their shoelaces in Reef-bows and Girls do so with 'Granny'-bows.
It is, in both cases, a question of proper seamanlike thinking/drinking.
Add hot water to Bovril and you have a nourishing drink.
Do the same to Marmite and you will probably be sick.
Anyway, **Captain Robert Falcon Scott** took Bovril with him to the Antarctic – not Marmite.

What you will also need

-A Lifeboat.
-A helicopter.
-A large piece of tin-foil.
-A zip-lock bag.
-A VHF radio set.
-A pair of binoculars.

Method

-Spread one piece of the bread with the Lurpak butter and smear with Shiphams Paste.
-Place upon it the Spam or other prepared-meat substance/substitute; season with the mustard and coat with the Sandwich spread and the Branston pickle.
-Butter one side of the second piece of bread and place butter side down on the meat melange.
-Now butter the other side of the bread and also the third slice.
-Onto the second slice spread the honey and jam and add slices of banana*.
-Coat the third slice with Bovril.
-Place the third slice on top to form a double-decker sandwich.
-Carefully wrap the sandwich in the tin-foil, but in a robust way and put into the zip-lock bag.
-Sit on the package to flatten it and reduce its size and then zip-it-locked.

Note: when eaten, it is quite delicious and obviates the necessity of keep things separate, and assuages the subsequent disappointment when they are not.
* Some people also add tinned peach slices at this stage but perhaps that is taking things a little too far.

Why do I need a Lifeboat? – I hear you ask

Well, here's what you do:

-Arrange to rendezvous with the (as was then) *'RNAS Lossiemouth' (HMS FULMAR)* air/sea rescue helicopter in order to carry out winching exercises with the Cromarty Lifeboat.

-Put to sea **in** the Cromarty Lifeboat and, reaching the rendezvous position, wait for the helicopter to turn up.

-Establish contact with the helicopter using the VHF radio set; the conversation proceeding something after this fashion:

"Hello, Cromarty Lifeboat. We see you and will be with you shortly."

"Hello, Helo. We do not see you but will be ready when you arrive."

After a bit.

"OK, Cromarty Lifeboat. We shall start the winch drills now."

"Where are you?"

"Well, we are right above you."

"No you're not. I do not see you."

Use binoculars to make certain.

"But you are waving at us."

"We certainly are not."

"Look, I'm winching my crewman down onto you now."

"Can't see you." (use sing-song intonation here.)

"But he's there with you. He's eating one of your sandwiches."

"Oh, I'm getting fed up with this. I am going back in. I don't know with whom you are operating - but it ain't us. Out!"

Return to Cromarty in high dudgeon.

Things to do afterwards

Write a letter to the Moray Outward-bound Sea School asking them to change the colour scheme of their venerable sailing-lifeboat to something different from the traditional RNLI paint job and thus avoid confusion.
Ask them what is so special about their sandwiches – thus securing the recipe.

Note: two lifeboats and a helicopter also make a fine sandwich.

-o0o-

The sixth one

GOZO GREEN-CAKE EXPERIMENTAL SNACK

Description

This is another recipe from the early 70s and was part of a group of dietary experiments carried out as part of '*The Great Gozo Expedition*' - from Malta GC to the island of Comino.

Other ongoing experiments included the efficacy of a purely salami diet on bicycle riding ability, coupled with the extension of food intake to include variations of the rough, red wine of the area (a brew inferior to 'Marsavin' – but freely available throughout the islands).

It was noted that the more obscure the wine container was, the rougher became the content, and the less able the subject was to proceed in an orderly manner bicycle-wise. This culminated in a draught served from a five gallon, aluminium, 'pusser's teapot - which quite did for the recipient.

The experiment was finalized on the return part of the journey with the 'Green Cake' incident.

Ingredients

-A 'green-cake', consisting of a cake-base surmounted by a 'pear', made of over-sweet, butter-sugar and iced in a virulent green colour.

-A large 'tot' of...
"King Henry the Eighth – finest Scoch Wiskey – produce of Gozo"

What you will need

-A partially willing experimentee/victim (in this case the 'Omelette Midshipman', by now promoted to Lieutenant.)
-A Chief Petty Officer Clearance Diver of villainous appearance (aren't they all?)
-Passage on the Malta-Gozo-Comino-Malta Ferry.
-Rough weather.

Method

-Place the experimentee/victim in the main saloon of the Gozo Ferry, along with the CPO Clearance Diver; but leave the bicycles on deck as they are not needed for this, preliminary, part of the test.
-Have the CPO examine the Saloon cake-counter for the most virulent and suspect form of confectionary he can find. Inevitably this will be the infamous 'green-cake', as nothing has ever surpassed it in respect of the required 'dodgy' appearance.
-He should then purchase this comestible, along with the required accompaniment of a large 'tot' of locally produced whiskey.
-Apply both these items internally to the victim and attempt to distract him fully from their consequence, and

the effects of the weather, for the half hour until docking at
Cirkewwa, Malta-side.
-On landing, observe the effects on the bicycle-riding
ability of the victim and assist where necessary.

At this point the experiment will necessarily have to be
terminated and the problem of conveying the experimentee
to a safe haven must be addressed.

-o0o-

Note of possible confusion – how to avoid it

The **next four recipes** are not of an edible type. However they are instructions of a similar nature and have therefore been collated into this RN section.
Enter with an open mind.

The first of four

POTENTATE'S CELEBRATION CAIKE

Description

This is an expensive, multi-layered confectionary that requires many years of preparation but, when executed, may be completed in a very short time.
In essence it concerns the demonstration of 'naval firepower' to the Potentate of a Middle Eastern country on the occasion of his birthday.

Preparation

You will need to acquire for yourself the formal accreditation of an Accountant. Do not bother to delve too deeply into the subject or else you may inadvertently come to possess an enhanced working knowledge and with it a position in British Commence or Industry; in which case you may have to actually work for a living.

Meanwhile, and you cannot start this too soon, ensure that you develop an over-bearing attitude to your work that will brow-beat people into following your lead and thus avoid unnecessary explanation or justification.

Once you have your accountancy certification, apply for the position of Head of Finance in a Middle Eastern country's Ministry of Defence, specifically within its Navy. Ensure that you avoid all contact with military or maritime forces up to this time. Any knowledge as to their workings would only cloud your thinking.

Establish yourself in the job, keeping your colleagues on their toes by being unpredictable and impossible to pin down, while ensuring that they experience the greatest difficulty in obtaining finances, through you, to achieve their set tasks. (A good tip here is to engender the requirement for endless 'justification-paperwork' from them to explain why they must have what you are supposed to be supplying to them in the first place in order to carry out their assigned tasks.)

Find yourself a suitable colleague in the Operations Department at Head Quarters who is senior enough to brook no argument yet not sufficiently astute to know what he is doing. (Not hard to find these days.)

Wait for the appropriate occasion to apply this recipe.

Ingredients

-One wooden-lattice, Naval gunnery target suitable for being towed behind a ship; cost: €5,200.
-Half a mile of towing hawser to facilitate the above; cost €1,300.

Total cost: €6,500.

Method

Once the opportunity has been identified – on this occasion, the Potentate's birthday celebrations – you will have to work fast as time is of the essence and, in order to keep people on their toes, you should not begin preparations too early.

-First; arrange to purchase the towed-target from a neighbouring country who's Navy is very much larger than yours and who have an abundance of spare targets of the type required.
-Second; arrange to purchase a towing hawser, it does not matter what type as long as it is half a mile long. If offered a floating one, go for it – it sounds good; however make sure that you go for the lowest 'tender', in true administrative fashion. Should an 'operator' (who will probably know what he is talking about) dare to suggest that this is not a suitable piece of rope – pull rank and ignore him.

-Third; arrange for your Operations colleague to have the items delivered to the participating Naval forces just before they are required; thus allowing too little time for the users to discover that they might not be entirely suitable. The pressure will be on by then and they will have to use what they are given.

-Fourth; pass the whole purchase over to your staff to pay for the items in the local currency of the donor country.

-Fifth; sit back in the knowledge of another task well done and wait for the accolades.

Things that may go wrong

-Your Staff may interpret the purchase price of 500,000 Rupees as 500,000 units of your own country's much stronger currency and, because the designated identification letter of that currency ('R') is the same as one of yours, they may pay that amount in **your** money - converted to the donor's local currency. Oops!

-If this occurs, watch carefully what you sign or you will end up paying the equivalent of €1,250,000 for a lump of wood and a long piece of string. Having received the money, it is doubtful that the donor Navy will apprise you of the mistake.

-The captain of the towing vessel may inform HQ that the towing hawser, although it floats very prettily, is of incorrect material and construction* for the task and liable to over-stretch and ultimately fail. Make sure that your

Operations colleague tells him to *'...wind his neck in'* and just get on and do what he is told.
*(material - 'polypropylene'; construction – 'hawser-laid' instead of the properly correct 'braided'.)

-Due to the necessity of allowing the Potentate a clear view of the fall of shot at the target, the firing range will have to be reduced and, consequently, the target is liable to be blown out of the water. When this occurs, the sudden release of the over-stretched towing hawser will cause it to tie itself in knots and tighten up into an un-recoverable mess – or, as the Navy has it, *'a bunch of bastards'*. The heat generated by this action will destroy the rope's buoyant qualities, causing it to sink to the bottom of the ocean while the matchwood remains of the target, its superstructure destroyed by the effective gunnery bombardment and its sponsons awash, will float away to the horizon as a *'...danger to shipping'*.
Don't worry about this; it will become someone else's problem.

How you can recover from this

As the evidence of the towed target is either at the bottom of the sea or dispersed by the waves, there will be nothing tangible to connect you to the event. However there are certain steps you can take to ensure your anonymity.

1. Speak enthusiastically about how successful the firepower demonstration turned out to be and how pleased

the Potentate was with it. By evoking this connection you will divert any possible speculation regarding the facts of the case.

2. Recover the financial over-spend by limiting the operational stores and support given to the Fleet, citing the necessity for economy in the worsening global financial climate.

3. Ensure that such economies do not apply to senior officers.

4. Never mention towed gunnery targets again.

-o0o-

The second of four

ROYAL NAVAL DRILL FOR DRINKING A PINT OF BEER

Description

This is the approved method of instructing a class of
sailors in the drill for 'drinking a pint of beer'.
As the squad of men will be some thirty yards distant, it
will require clear diction, an ability to project the voice
over the intervening interval in a clear and precise manner.
It will also require the 'eagle-eye', as of a parade-staff
Drill Instructor.

Ingredients

-A squad of about a dozen or more sailors or, if they are
available, Midshipmen. These last are more fun to play
with.

What you will need

-A Parade-ground.
-The use of a Petty Officer Gunnery Instructor (POGI or
just 'GI'). They are the world's experts in the drilling of
men).
-A very loud voice; clear and precise (as previously stated)
and the 'brass neck' to do the job properly, without let or
hindrance nor showing any favouritism whatsoever.

-If available, the facilities of the Whale Island Naval Gunnery School – just for kicks.

Method

-Stand in the middle of the tarmac parade ground, with the squad of men some thirty yards away, and follow this simple procedure:

One: Secure the attention of the squad, sort out any misbehaviour (doesn't matter if there isn't any – invent it) and settle them down.

Two: Divide the action up into its component parts and run through it 'by numbers' (making sure to rectify any mistakes, real or imaginary, as you go).

Three: Practice the squad in the whole drill until they've learned it properly.

Four: Keep it as simple as possible.

Using your best parade-ground voice, proceed as follows: (Note: words in **bold type** should be given with particular emphasis and volume.)

*"**Squad!** Squad ... **HAAH!** By – the – right ... **DRESS!** Number three, front rank, get your arm horizontal to the deck.*
Brace-up, number two.

*Squad ... eyes **FRONT!** Stand at **EASE!** Stand easy."*

(Right, that's the 'start-up-bit' over with and you have their attention. Now, cease 'shouting' and, instead, use the staccato, sing-song GI's voice but with stacks of volume.)

"Detail for drinking a pint of beer.
*At the order '**One**', the starboard forearm is moved smartly to a position pointing directly ahead, with the arm bent at the elbow to form a right angle between the fore and upper arm.*
The forearm should be parallel to the deck, the hand grasping the pint mug in a vice-like grip; after this fashion."

(Demonstrate this with an imaginary pint glass (with handle for officers; without handle for sailors) held in the right hand.)

*"**Squad!** Brace yourselves. Properly at ease. Squad ...*
HAAH! – DON'T SWAY!
Squad, detail for drinking a pint of beer – by numbers.
*Squad – **ONE!***
Hold those arms steady.
*I can see you moving at the back there. **Stand still!***
Second rank, first man; that's a pint pot you're supposed to be holding – not a dinky little cocktail glass.
Rear rank, end man, get your heels together and straighten that back."

*"At the order '**Two**', the starboard arm is brought smartly up and turned through ninety degrees with both fore and upper arm parallel to the deck, the thumb resting between the lower lip and the chin; - thus."*

(Once again, demonstrate this movement but adjust the position of the imaginary pint glass depending on whether it is held with the hand enveloping it or grasping the handle.)

*"Squad – **TWO!***
Get those elbows up!
*You're supposed to be about to drink from it, number four, front rank, not look into it. **Get your head up!**"*

*"At the order '**Three**', the hand grasping the pint mug is tilted toward the mouth at an angle of forty-five degrees, the lips forming a firm seal around the rim.*
Waiting a pause of two marching paces, a pre-determined portion of the glass content is then swallowed."

*"Squad – **THREE!** Up – two, three – swallow – two, three – STOP!**
When I say 'swallow – two, three – stop', I mean you to stop, not drain the whole glass and ask for another pint - - Mr Brothers!
*As you were; return to the designated attitude. **Do it again!***
*Squad – **THREE!** Up – two, three – swallow – two, three – STOP!*

That's better."

*"Now, at the order '****Four****', the starboard arm is restored to its previous position, vis-à-vis the order 'One', namely with the forearm at ninety degrees to both the upper arm and the body, parallel to the deck and pointing ahead, the glass still clutched in a vice-like grip by the hand – thus."*

*"Squad – ****FOUR!**** And ****move it!****
Right. Stand still; don't sway.
That wasn't too bad but I want to see a bit more snap to it.
Try it again."*

*"Squad, by numbers, drinking a pint of beer, -- ****ONE!****
(two, three), ****TWO!**** (two, three), ****THREE!**** (two, three),
****DRINK**** (two, three), ****SWALLOW**** (two, three) and ****FOUR!****
STAND STILL!!"*

*"Not at all bad. You've all been practising, obviously.
Right, now we'll try it as one drill movement, dwelling a
pause of two marching paces between each step."*

*"Squad, one pint of beer – ****DRINK!**** Up – two, three –
Over – two, three – Tilt – two, three – Swallow – two,
three – Down and ****still!****
Stand at – ****EASE!**** Stand easy."*

(It is at this point that the POGI you have borrowed from Whale Island Parade Staff might interject with a comment.)

"Most impressive, Mr. Ottery. I think you're a natural born actor and mimic. For a moment there I thought it was the Chief of the Parade doin' the shouting.
Right, double away and rejoin the squad.
Mr Brothers get out here an' give the detail for 'tying a shoe lace'. **AT THE DOUBLE**, *you 'orrible, low-life kay-det; an' I hope someone gives you as much grief as you gave your oppo."*

Glossary of terms

"HAAH!"   "Attention!"
"DRESS!"   "Sort yourselves out into straight lines, both fore and aft."
Deck.   Any flat surface upon which men stand.
Stand at ease.   Legs apart (athwart-ships), hands clasped behind the back.
Stand easy.   As 'Stand at ease' but in a slightly more relaxed attitude.
Starboard arm.   Right arm.
Mr Ottery.   The man in charge of the drill (- *in my mind!*)
Mr Brothers.   Someone else.
Kay-det.   Cadet – the lowest form of animal life – before they became
                    slightly elevated to the rank of
Midshipmen.
Oppo.   Particular chum.
-o0o-

The third of four

HOW TO RIDE A HORSE

Introduction

At the end of the 19th century, during the Boer War, a Naval Brigade was landed from the supporting Royal Navy warships in order to reinforce the Army in land operations against the enemy. In this they proved to be resourceful and very effective, achieving legendary status and great renown.

One of their tasks was to transport field artillery over difficult terrain, where, because of cliffs and chasms, mule teams were not able to operate. Thus it was left to the sailors themselves to convey the guns to their destination. This feat of pure seamanship and unrelenting endurance has been commemorated since those heroic days by the annual competition at the commencement Earl's Court 'Royal Tournament' – which is the Field Gun Race – between teams from the dockyard ports of Chatham, Plymouth Portsmouth and from the Fleet Air Arm. Sadly, due to defence cuts and the topsy-turvy juxtaposition that exists between military expenditure and national heritage, this magnificent example of what ordinary sailors can achieve with proper training and boundless enthusiasm is now long gone and you will never see the like again.

Another major problem to be solved in the South African war was how to transport the urgently needed troops of the Naval Brigade speedily to their destination.

Motor transport not then being in viable existence, the horse was the only alternative and this was the last time such a massive naval troop movement was achieved in this fashion. However there was a major obstacle to be overcome; that of teaching the sailors how to ride their horses – a skill completely outside their accomplishments at that time.

Ever resourceful in these matters and with the dictum *'There is nothing the British Tar cannot achieve with the proper training and drill'* firmly in mind, the Royal Navy turned to its Gunnery Branch (responsible for all such matters) for a solution.

The result was a celebrated piece of 'drill' that has achieved almost mythical repute; although few people have ever had the chance to actually see the document. No doubt it languishes deep in some dusty archive, unwanted, unused and unappreciated, to go the way of all good things Navy and disappear into obscurity, never to be seen again.

However, there is hope.

Any person who has been adequately trained in the ways of the parade ground, naval drill and proper seamanship will be able to emulate those long gone Gunnery and Seamanship Instructors of the Fleet and reproduce in some form the essence of *'...how to teach a sailor to ride a horse.'* All it requires is the will to do so.

Here then is the subject, taken and rendered as accurately as possible from the 1970s; for we are all old, now, and such memories are the only comfort we have left.
Forget your 21st century way of thinking, cluttered as it is by microchips and X-boxes and everything made of plastic. Think back to the last days of that older Navy before the disappearance of the sailing whaler, spun-yarn, oars, canvas, mess-deck-scrubbers, navy-cake and Kai. Return again half a century and tackle the problem from that perspective.

Description

The Chief Gunnery Instructor addresses a muster of sailors:

"Right! Pay attention this way and stand properly at ease. Right? Right! Stand easy."

"The object of today's lecture is to acquaint you with the Horse and the proper drill for riding the animal. Now, I am aware that many of you may never have come in contact with the equine mode of transport before but you all know your seamanship and you all know boats. A Horse is no different from any small boat or skiff and, if properly handled by the correct drill, will cause you no problems. Right? Right!"

"The first thing you will notice about the Horse is the height of the beast and the fact that it has four legs. Do not let this worry you. It is no higher than the boat lying on deck in its chocks. Anything below the waterline is quite simply subject to the arrangements for steering and propulsion that is controlled from the Cockpit."

"The Horse has a Bow and a Stern, just like a boat, and a Port and Starboard side as well. So you will be quite at home in that respect. A major difference, however, is that the Horse's steering arrangements are forward. Instead of a tiller you have a pair of Yoke-lines leading to the Figurehead, which you may regard as taking the place of the rudder. Also the Keel is on the top of the animal, running from the Figurehead to the Stern-sheets (where, incidentally, a passenger may be carried) and from it is suspended the Hull. The Ribs of the Hull are attached to the Keel just as in any normal boat; the only difference being that, as with anything connected to the Cavalry, everything is about-face, topsy-turvy and upside-down - and the propulsion is from below the waterline instead of aloft."

"Although there is no actual Cockpit in a Horse, there is a leathern Mollgogger secured athwart ships, with a Belly-band running from one side of the Hull to the other and adjusted for tension by a leather tackle secured by straps. Attached to this are two Lizards, one to port and the other to starboard, with large Thimbles into which the feet are put. Thus you will be sitting on the thwart and safely held

there by your feet in these devices – which those of you familiar with square-rig sailing will recognise as Stirrups – which indeed they are."

What you will need

"For cox'n'ing this craft, normal No. 2 square-rig uniform is to be worn but with boots, gaiters and webbing belt. Caps will have chin-stays down.
No.1 rig is to be worn on ceremonial occasions only."

Marks of respect

"Normal marks of respect will be paid to all officers and to this end the Yoke-lines should be held in the left hand to facilitate proper saluting with the right."

Executive orders

"There are only two Executive Orders that are given to the Horse and they are:

'Giddy-up there!' *and* 'Whoa, Dobin!'

"Executive Order No.1 'Giddy-up there!' is the order for the Horse to proceed in a forward direction. It may be repeated when a change of speed is required.
Executive Order No. 2 'Whoa, Dobbin!' is the order for the Horse to slow down and eventually to come to a halt."

"There is one further exclamation that may be used to soothe, comfort or praise the Horse, if it should be deemed necessary. Using a conciliatory tone of voice and, while patting the Horse's neck, say, 'Good horsey.'
Only these three orders may be given and that is all you need to know at this stage."

Method

"First, ensure that the belly-band that secures the Mollgogger to the Hull is sufficiently tight. This is done by taking the straps of the adjusting-tackle in hand, raising the knee sharply into the vicinity of the lower hull-strakes, causing the Horse to exhale sharply. This will allow you to secure an extra notch or two in the tightening mechanism to make the standing rigging properly taut."

1. Stepping aboard.
"Stand on the Port side of the Horse, facing inboard, with the Yoke-lines in the left hand. Place the left foot into the Thimble of the Port Stirrup. Grasp the starboard-after edge of the Mollgogger with the right hand and use it to assist when stepping aboard. Step up onto the left foot, raising the body and twisting it to face forward, at the same time lifting the right leg high over the Stern-sheets and swing it down to the starboard side, while releasing your right hand to fall naturally alongside the right thigh. Sit upon the leather Mollgogger-thwart and slide the right foot into the Thimble of the Starboard Lizard (stirrup)."

2. *Disembarking.*

"With the left hand holding the Yoke-lines, use it to take a firm grasp of the starboard-forward edge of the Mollgogger. Loosen the right foot from the Starboard Stirrup and swing the leg up and over the Stern-sheets until all the weight of the body is supported by the left leg. At the same time, straighten the left leg so that the body is upright and facing inboard.

Now step down, removing the left foot from the Port Lizard thimble on completion, to leave you facing the horse in the at-ease position.

This action should be accomplished in a simple, fluid motion in order to cause as little anxiety to the Horse as possible. Do not jump down from the Mollgogger as such feats are the preserve of Circus performers and race-horse jockeys – neither of which you are!"

3. *Casting-off and getting under way.*

"Having boarded the craft, settle in position and grasp the Yoke-lines firmly in both hands, at about chest height. The following three actions should be carried out simultaneously:

a) give the Yoke-lines a snap forward with the wrists in a flicking motion.

b) swing both heels back and inwards to give a sharp jolt to the lower Hull-strake.

c) give the executive order, 'Giddy-up there!'

The Horse will start off at a slow and steady pace. Further speed advantages may be obtained by repeating the process; as will be explained later."

4. *Heaving-to and berthing.*
*"Heaving-to is achieved by pulling the Yoke-lines gently
but firmly astern and giving the executive order,* 'Whoa,
Dobbin!' *The Horse will then come to a stop and
disembarking can be carried out.*
*This method is also used to take in a reef and slow down
forward speed. In an emergency the Yoke-lines should be
pulled astern more forcefully by leaning the upper body aft
and swinging the legs toward the Bow. The Executive
Order should be given in a more forceful manner. Extreme
emergency may be countered by carrying out the above
procedure with more vigour and raising the voice to a
stentorian roar."*

5. *Steering and tacking.*
*"The Yoke-line may be hauled aft on the Starboard side to
turn the craft in that direction or on the Port side to
achieve that distinction. The greater the force used, the
tighter will be the turn and, unfortunately, the more
fractious will become the Horse. It is recommended that,
as in sailing, these changes in direction be made in a calm
and gentle manner or else a capsize will be almost
inevitable."*

6. *Taking in and shaking out reefs.*
"The Horse has four speeds:
Close-hauled*; proceeding at a leisurely pace, comfortably
and without shipping water.*

Full-and-by; sailing somewhat faster with a choppy motion that is uncomfortable in the extreme and liked neither by the Horse nor its Cox'n. It should be avoided as far as possible.

Beam-reaching; a good speed for covering distance and control is more finite in its application. This can be maintained for considerable periods but should be alternated with running 'close-hauled' from time to time.

Running-free; the fastest it is possible to go but where control is minimal and early reefing is advised."

"To increase speed, or to shake-out reefs, the procedure for 'Getting under way' should be followed at each augment of speed required, using Executive Order No. 1 exclusively.

To reduce speed, or take-in reefs, the procedure for 'Heaving-to' should be followed as each reduction is required, using Executive Order No. 2 in similar manner. Upon successful reefing it is recommended that the procedure for complimenting the Horse be used – 'Good horsey.' "

Hints

"In order to ensure close co-operation between the Horse and the Cox'n, half-apples (if available) or sugar lumps should be given regularly – either way is recommended but never both at the same time."

"When passing astern of the Horse, it is advisable to do so as close to the transom as possible, thus avoiding the possibility of kick-back from a disgruntled beast."

"Cleaning the hull with a short-haired brush will keep the craft looking spruce. Always remember that, as '...a Ship is known by her Boats', the Naval Brigade is known by its Horses."

"Make sure that you keep them happy and well looked after at all times; and make sure to return them to Stores in good condition."

Glossary

Field Gun Race
The most extreme form of physical competition in the world.
Fleet Air Arm
The Navy that Flies.
Cockpit
Position in a boat where the Cox'n holds sway and the tiller.
Cox'n
The sailor in charge of the boat and its crew.
Bow
The front of a boat.
Stern
The back of a boat.
Port

A haven from a storm and a delightful drink to celebrate the fact.

Starboard

The side of a boat that is over there (to the right facing forr'd).

Tiller

A piece of fore-n-aft wood that acts on the rudder to turn the craft. It can also be a form of high-kicking female woman of the opposite sex.

Rudder

The board that hangs vertically in the water to regulate direction.

Yoke-lines

Pieces of rope that join the two (above) when they are 'remote'.

Keel

The 'backbone' of the craft or, for a Horse, just its backbone.

Stern-sheets

Doubles as the Cockpit (q.v.) and a space for carrying spare officers.

Hull

A watertight carapace that prevents the occupants from drowning.

Ribs

Those which give the Hull grace – which passes all understanding.

Cavalry

Not the Horse Marines; a land-based equivalent, but *with* horses.

Mollgogger
A smooth, leather-covered fair-lead, sometimes used for sitting upon.
Belly-band
The broad canvas or leather strap that keeps a stowed craft in place.
Lizard
A pendant that has spliced into one extremity a metal 'hoop' or Thimble.
Chin-stay
The woven band that passes under the chin to prevent loss of a cap.
Heave-to
Contrive to have the sailing boat stationary – while still sailing.
Reef
Reduce speed by gathering in some sail - to make it smaller.

-o0o-

The fourth of four

HEIST SOUFLE

Although not RN, this is another inedible recipe - but a fine one to end this section.

Description.

In order to obtain money, it is necessary to have a job.
In order to obtain more money, it is necessary to either take a second job or to work harder, longer, more diligently at the one you already have.
In order to obtain more money quickly, it will be necessary to either:

> Gamble on the horses;
> Sell the sofa and other selected pieces of furniture;
> Take out a loan;
> Rob a Bank.

This last may seem rather drastic but, in these days of comparative lawfulness, not many people are doing it. Therefore the advantage of surprise is all the more apparent.

Ingredients

You will need:
-One or two accomplices to assist you
-Some form of disguise

-A large bag to hold the loot
-Authentic-looking 'replica' pistols to encourage someone
to open the vault
-A 'get-away' car
-A 'get-away' driver to pilot the 'get-away' car
-Some coins for the parking meter

Note: It is recommended that the 'get-away' car should be
powerful, nondescript and nimble. It is further
recommended that the escape route be surveyed in advance
to facilitate swift and easy egress from the scene and that
the time chosen be as quiet as possible, in relation to
passers-by.

Method
Or, in this case, **'How Not to Do It'**.

-Do not choose a Cornish country town on Market Day.
-Do not select for the 'get-away' a large, American car that
is painted in a virulent pink and yellow, two-tone design.
-Do not cruise around the Market Square until a parking
space is available opposite the Bank of choice.
-Do not bother to pay for a parking ticket; you should not
be there long enough for it to matter.
-Do not don your Clown-mask disguises in the car before
you have selected your parking slot; someone will notice.
Wait until entering the Bank.
-Do not roughly shove spectators aside on your way to the
Bank. They are only trying to enjoy what is perceived to
be a Carnival atmosphere.

On exiting the Bank, carrying your loot:
-Do not simply get back into the car and expect to drive off. It is quite possible that an elderly lady, intent on a quick visit to Boots Chemist, will have temporarily parked across the front of the 'get-away' car, rendering it immobile and you inside it (still wearing your clown masks) liable to arrest from the extra Police Officers normally attendant in the Town Square on Market Day.

Historical note. This is a true story and worthy of all men to be believed. If ever you go to Launceston (capital town of Cornwall), have a look at the Market Square and try to work out which of the four high-street banks was the target.

-o0o-

STUDENT DAYS

For all who, perhaps, do not remember those 'halcyon' times (when the best of us had difficulty boiling water without burning it), here is a small 'squint'* to jog the memory. *['squint' "...an oblique opening through the wall ... affording a view of the – (whatever)....]

RECIPES FOR DISASTER -- or Dishes of Desperation

"Leave undone those things that you ought to have done and do those things that you ought not to have done: that is a Recipe for Disaster."

Description

Using your own, personal time-machine (your imagination), transport yourself back to The Summer of Love (1967) when some of us were at sea, earning an honest(if somewhat salt-sprayed) crust, and others were pioneering Psychedelic Light Shows with such luminaries as **'The Animals', 'Jimmy Hendrix', 'The Cream'** and **'The Nice'** – among others – Who? Well, yes, **'The Who', 'The Crazy World of Arthur Brown'** *["I am the God of Hell-fire; and I bring you FIRE!!"]*, **'The Small Faces'** and **'Judy Driscoll and the Brian Augur Trinity'** et al . (Note: it was great fun but there was no money in either of these pursuits.)

In this latter case, imagine yourself to be young, free and without a care in the world – apart from where the next meal is to be found.

You have returned to your 'grotty bed-sit' [authentic 60s' slang] in the attic of a decrepit Victorian terrace somewhere off Birmingham's Pershore Road after a night's creative Light-showing (and, believe me, they were exhausting). Having climbed the many stairs, you finally sit down, hungry and exhausted, looking at the scant provision of specie in your hand. [We're talking serious lack of money here.]

What you will need

-A certain amount of creative imagination.

-What money you have in your hand at the time or can glean from sofas, armchairs, telephone boxes (press button B) or the nearest ornamental fountain*.

-The four recipes below.

* Note: I was always surprised by the predilection the general public had/has for throwing coins into fountains. Then it occurred to me that this was to feed the 'water sprites' (in this case - a penniless 'me', at night with a small net) in the hopes that they would be granted a good wish. Well, they have and always have had my very best good wishes – especially after I had eaten.)

-o0o-

Recipe One

PORK AND CHOCOLATE PIE

Ingredients

-A bus-stop
-Two four-and-a-half-penny pork pies (small – very small, and only nine-pence in old [real] money)
-One old six-penny bar of Cadbury's milk chocolate (old money - that is)
-Two measures of rain and one of regret

Method

-Approach the bus-stop late at night, in the rain and in the forlorn hope that the last bus has yet to arrive.
-Wait for a time until the forlorn hope has dissolved into regret and there remains nothing but a hunger for ...... food of any kind ... now!
-Take one of the pork-pies, together with half of the chocolate bar and cram them into your mouth wholesale. (They make up a single mouthful between them.)
-Chew with the regret, aware that the last bus has long gone and you will have to walk home in leaky shoes. [The days had not yet arrived when all young people appeared to wear chunky boots.]
-Save the remaining pork-pie and half -bar of chocolate for the same time tomorrow, when.....   -Repeat the process.

(Historical note: this recipe was developed during a particularly hard, cold, wet winter in Manchester.)
-o0o-

Recipe Two

PORRIDGE IN A DRAWER

What you will need

-Porridge
-An army-surplus chest of drawers containing.....
-A drawer
-A Bakelite knife – but only if you have one; any other kind of knife will do almost as well
-Some kind of container – a large, galvanized bucket would be fine
-A stirring device
-Two matches

Ingredients

-A large quantity of rough (i.e. cheap) porridge-oats or their equivalent.
(**Note**: if you are using this recipe, you will not be choosy.)
-Water – you will not be able to get 'Pussers' water, so don't even try.
-Salt or sugar - or even both; whatever is to hand, really, but don't use other white crystals such as Alum or Harpic – they do nothing for the dish.

Method

-Put the ingredients into the bucket and stir it into a consistency.
-Place the bucket onto the communal gas-ring on the landing and feed the last of your money to the gas-meter.
-Use one of the matches to light the burner. (Save the other for emergencies.)
-Leave the gas on 'very low'.

Now remove your underwear and socks – from the drawer!

Historical note: In the 1960s, the Royal Navy's Diving Manual contained the following instruction:
"The practice of determining the fortitude of candidates by removing their underwear is to be discouraged."
So, keep yours on!

-Clean the drawer of fluff and dust – or use these as flavouring.
-Once the porridge is cooked or when the gas runs out, pour the content of the bucket into the drawer and allow it to cool.
-Return the bucket to the coal-cellar whence you borrowed it.
-Replace the drawer into its accustomed place.

Serving suggestions and Safety

With the knife, cut out a suitable portion of the solidified porridge for the day and put it in your pocket for later.

This recipe should last you for a week at the least – or more if frugal.

Beware of scurvy!

-oOo-

Recipe Three

MEAT IN A BAG

What you will need

-Some kind of heat-proof tray – or trays.
-The 'Baby Belling' cooker on the downstairs landing.
-A bag
-A sharp knife (optional). (Observation: if your knife is not sharp, you may as well use a hammer!)
-Enough change to 'feed the meter'.

Ingredients

-The cheapest cuts of meat that the butcher will let you have. Ask him for 'scrag-end of sheep'. It is about as cheap a cut as you will find.*
-Salt, if you have any.

*Fast-forward fifty years and you will come across new problems. Depending upon the part of the country in which you find yourself, the butcher will either refuse to serve you as, he will say, *"...we are 'high class' butchers; we do not sell cheap cuts!"*; or he will offer you *'hilal'* meat and charge you accordingly.
However, 'neck of lamb' might still be found at a reasonable price.

Method

-Cut up the meat into very thin strips with the knife. You can save yourself the trouble if the butcher is a kind-hearted fellow and agrees to butcher it for you – after all, it is his job.

-Place the meat strips on the tray or trays and carry them to the down-stairs landing where the 'Baby Belling' (oven-and-two-hot-plates) is situated.

-Make sure that you have previously agreed with the other 'bed-sit' occupants for them not to use the 'Baby Belling' until you have finished. They will be quite OK with this as they have either been in, are currently in or are glad not to be in the same situation as that in which you find yourself.

-Insert as much change as you need/have/can afford into the meter.

-Put the tray or trays into the oven and turn the heat onto its lowest possible setting.

-Wait.

Note: The object here is to dry the meat, not to cook it. Dried meat is *good* and part of the recipe. Cooked meat is *not good* as it does not keep for very long and eventually becomes rotten. (Then all you can do is to curry it – which is rather beyond the remit of these recipes.)

-When the meat is dry (or after your money has run out), bring it back upstairs to cool on the window ledge. (Warning: if it is raining – do not do this or you will have soggy meat which will go-off something horrid.)

-Once the meat is cold, put it into the bag and close.

Serving suggestions and Safety

Before you go to work, put the bag into your pocket. During the day, fish-out small pieces of the dried meat and chew – and chew – and chew.

Once again - beware of scurvy!

-o0o-

Recipe Four

ORIGINAL 'BURGOO!'

What you will need

-A bucket – probably the one you used before.
-The other match – <u>this is the emergency for which you saved it</u>.
-A gas-ring or any other heat-source – several candle stubs will just about do if you have no other option.
- Gas-meter-change.
In fact, all the usual essentials for Desperation Dishes.

Ingredients

-The remaining contents of the porridge drawer.
-The residue of the meat from the bag.
-Anything edible left in the vicinity of the 'bed-sit' cooking stations. Your fellow housemates will doubtless donate their left-overs to you if you have reached this stage and they feel 'flush'.
-Some water.

Method

-After a final foray to the nearest fountain, take the change you have acquired, dry it and feed it into the gas-meter.
-Fetch the bucket from the coal cellar and give it a wipe out.

-Scrape the remains of the porridge from the drawer and empty what you get, plus the residue from the meat-bag, into the bucket.

-To this add whatever donations or food remnants you have been able to garner and stir the whole lot up with the water.

-Light the gas with the remaining match.

-Bring to the boil and allow to simmer until anything nasty that might be contained therein is long dead and inert; or until the gas runs out.

Serving suggestion
Just eat it out of the bucket with a spoon.

Hopeful hint
This is probably the last meal you will have to scrimp - as things will probably get better tomorrow.

-o0o-

RECIPES FROM THE MAZAUDET COOK-BOOK
or
Simple Meals to share with Dogs

Our Wanderer has now come home to settle down; however, during his absence from the country of his birth, that land has changed considerably. Mediocrity (a quality he has spent his lifetime – so far – avoiding) has become the new *'good'* and his countrymen have been led into an apathy that is seldom stirred from the cosy inactivity of the TV couch. Not only that, but the *'cost of things'* has risen beyond that with which his carefully tended pension funds can cope.

So, it seems, he must venture abroad once more but, this time, on a permanent basis.
Where to go?
He settles on/in a part of France that is deeply 'rural'; where the sight of three cars on the road between his retreat and the nearest town, twenty kilometres away, heralds a busy day in the countryside.
It is a forested area, where oak and chestnut are long term 'crops' and where horses still work the woodland rides alongside more modern and terribly efficient forestry machinery. There are many Buzzards here, along with Eagle Owls, Red Squirrels, Deer and Wild Boar – all of

which enter the garden he is making from an old orchard. When it rains, it does so in Hollywood fashion and at times the wind can blow-up a storm that will up-root trees in abundance. In the summer it is really quite hot and the winters can reach 'twenty below'.

At the small hamlet, in which he lives - where the 'pave' ends, there is his ancient farmhouse and barns, with nothing beyond but field and forest and the start of a mighty French river. Among the out-buildings (most fallen into ruin) there remains an antediluvian cottage that was once the bake-house for the small settlement and now, equipped with a century-old, wood-burning 'range', has come back into its own as the *'Mazaudet Country Kitchen'*.

It is here, by the warmth of the fire, that the Traveller finally comes to rest and, in the time that passes at a leisurely pace, finally sets down his thoughts on what it is to be an Expat.

It is here that he can collate all that he has learned in his adventuring and can create the 'Guide to Expat Survival' that is this book.

It is here that the 'Mazaudet Cook Book' can take form.

For Mazaudet is the place where he has settled and which, in the tranquil environs of his new, yet ancient abode, he can finally call *'Home'*.

The Mazaudet Country Kitchen became almost world famous some years ago when it was awarded the coveted 'Three Michelan Oven Gloves' in recognition of its producing some of best, barely affordable meals in France.

Here is an extract from that first Michelan Guide correspondent:

"Mazaudet is where its 'Chef de Maison', the one-time explosives disposal expert/boxer/sailing-ship master, Bernie Bruen, creates and survives on some of the choicest of simple dishes, many of them described within the pages of this book. A tad malnourished perhaps, but he has suffered little harm so far! And there simply is no one I know who lives on a tighter budget than he.

"Mazaudet is a small hamlet in the country, a good day's walk south of Limogoes (famous for is radio station years ago; remember it?) Bernie's kitchen is in Mazaudet and therefore, 'in the country', which is how it came by its name; useful to know. Whenever I visit him, I am always amazed at how uncomplicated a life he leads and how simple and wholesome is his cooking. I swear I once witnessed him boiling grass clippings for soup, but then again he does own a variety of animals and fowl so I could have been mistaken. The soup may have been for them. Bernie's recipes are well thought out, yet simple, tasty and affordable enough to be included in this Guide. I have never seen him ponder over creating a meal. Like a distinguished painter who goes directly to his canvas and

starts sploshing paint around, Bernie has the innate ability to do the same with food ingredients, to cook it, and survive to tell the tale. (He goes for sepia-coloured ingredients mainly but does not lay them on canvas.)"

Recipe One

A GOOD BEEF STEW

Description

This recipe defies description, but as a rule of thumb, if the dogs eat it then it's deemed to be good. You may or may not know that, in France, dogs eat with the family. It is a tradition that defies logic but then, to their credit, Frenchmen and women never claimed to be logical. Farmhouses all over France are cooking this dish for their Sunday lunch prior to resting in front of the television to watch riveting games of 'boules'. We have chosen this ancient dish first as, unlike the majority of French *'cuisine cooking'* [as an acquaintance once had it], you do not have to use butter, creme-fraiche, duck fat or full-cholesterol cream – which will help you to keep your hour-glass figure or handsome appearance.

Ingredients

-A lump of the cheapest beef you can find (a *'promotion'* from your local French supermarket should do it). Don't worry about it being tough and fatty, the tenderness will come with the way you handle it.
-3 or 4 French onions.
-2 garlic cloves (especially if your hounds are looking at you in a slavering way. It works in much the same way as

with vampires; yet, surprisingly dogs love to eat it. It is all very confusing.).
-As many potatoes as you think accomplishes a 'fair portion'.   -1 big bay leaf.
-Any kind of bouillon stock you fancy (but you don't need to rob a bank to afford this meal).
-Goose grease by the handful.
-Flour 'ordinaire'.

What you may need besides

-A pressure cooker may help. (After all this is a 'pressure cooker recipe', as most of them seem to be.)
-A fire in a hearth, with a wrought-iron, three-legged cooking stand for absolute authenticity.
-A promising stomach.
-Some very hungry dogs.
-A wad of wire wool for cleaning the soot from the pressure cooker when finished.
-A tin of 'Gleem-o' or similar for polishing the pressure cooker when you have concluded the scrubbing of it.

Method:

-Taking the lump of the cheapest beef you could lay your hands on, cut into chunks (discard the bone – or not depending upon your mood swing at the time).

-Add to the meat three or four onions and a few bulbs of garlic.   -

Roughly peel the potatoes and cut into doggie shapes.

-Pour over all of this a rough pint of the bouillon stock of your choice (or half a litre of the finer stuff if you actually do live in France).

-Shovel the whole lot into the pressure cooker and place onto the stove.

-Add enough coal or logs to the fire to ensure that the following instruction may be complied with:

-Bring up to 5lbs pressure (or ten centimes in Metric) and cook thus for an hour and a half on a very low heat.

-When this has been completed, take equal amounts of goose-grease and flour, cook together for a few minutes (in a separate pan of course) and add the resulting mess to the stew and stir in. This will thicken the whole shebang almost immediately.

By the time you have thought about it, it will be ready for eating.

And jolly good it is too. *Patch** told me so. It's definitely a 'second helping' dish. You may even wish to try some yourself, or invite friends around with their dogs.

**Patch* – The dog from the farm next-door, who tended to hang around with our dogs – particularly at meal times.

-o0o-

Recipe Two

'EXCELLENT' CHICKEN STEW'

Description

This recipe is a very old French country house dish where only the best fresh ingredients were to be found. So if you want to replicate it, then you will need to do so 'without means' – (whatever that means).

Note; ('Excellent' remains silent in French.)

Ingredients

-Seven or eight best chicken thighs (or *'chicken thiggs'* as they are known at Mazaudet).
-A mushroom, one per person – no more!
-3 freshly dug onions.
-Several bulbs of freshly dug garlic.
-4 un-blighted potatoes.
-2 whole bay-shaped leaves and a generous handful of 'Herbs de Provence'. (Note: you do not have to go to 'Provence' to get them; they are available from 'Madame' next-door.)
-3 bouillon cubes of your choice (but we thing that chicken would do best).
-3 hand-picked apples (any EU franked apple shaped variety. Not those ugly foreign ones).

-A spoonfull of honey (*bees' honey* for the best results; in these EU days that's what it says on the label. We have searched in vain for other 'makes' of honey.)
-2 measures of the roughest French wine available.

What you may need besides

-A local French wine-seller or cellar.
-A pepper mill.
-Another pressure cooker. *

Method:

Put the following into the bottom of the pressure cooker:
-7 or 8 chicken-thigh-portions and a mushroom**.
-Add 3 onions (roughly chopped for a coarse finish or gently for a smooth one, it doesn't matter).
-3 unpeeled bulbs of garlic.
-The 4 potatoes (cut into squares – they must be cut into squares or else the whole ambience of the thing will be ruined and the local Mazaudetians will not be very polite when next they see you).
-Add the 2 bay-leaves at this time and the 3 picked apples cut into pieces of eight.

Into a jug place:
-The three bouillon cubes of indeterminate origin.
-2 table-spoons of honey. (Once again, only bees' honey will do. Wasp honey will not cut it and earwigs only make gravy – or so I am told.)

-1 teaspoonful of herbs*** (preferably from Provence – or your local corner shop if you don't happen to live in France).

-Some sea-salt. (Sorry! We forgot to list that; but I'm sure you will have some lying about somewhere – most people do.)

-Pepper from the pepper mill if you have one close to you.

-1 pint of hot water – or half a metre if you live in France. Mix it all up and pour into the pressure cooker.

For good fortune, add a good measure of the extremely rough red wine – the sort that takes the enamel off the teeth. (2 euros for 5 litres in your local French wine supermarket; but not to be found in the likes of M&S or Waitrose, no matter how diligently you may search.)

* It is your choice whether or not you remove the remains of yesterday's *'Good Beef Stew'* and scour the pot. It all depends on your preference for flavours.

** It is normal in France to have a complete thigh per person; they don't do things by halves – or do they?

*** If you are American – use *'erbs*.

Note; Although this is regarded as a high class French dish, the use of cheap wine is permissible owing to two factors;

(1) the current state of the Euro/Sterling exchange rate and (2) the fact that two hundred years ago all French wine was cheap. (I looked it up on Google.)

-Stoke up the fire with wood or coal and cook on a low heat at the usual 5lbs pressure for an hour and a half – well, maybe just for an hour, or less if you are that hungry. The resulting repast will be warming and satisfying and just the thing for a winter's day.

-o0o-

Recipe Three

BOEUF au NINDEL

Description:

Surprisingly, this is not a French recipe. It sounds so French, don't you think? But no, it is not and I will challenge anyone who disagrees to duel over the matter.

Ingredients:

-Beef of one kind or another, preferably from a cow.
-Spanish-speaking onions.
-Tinned tomatoes.
-Orange carrots (coloured, not flavoured).
-1 Golden Delicious - apple, that is (not a female of the opposite sex).

For the Sauce: (use only a silver rat's-tail spoon for measuring, not one of those stainless substitutes)

-Half an inch of Lee and Perrin's Celebrated Worcestershire Sauce.
-2 and a half tsp of Old Mother Wormold's Celebrated Curry Powder.
-3 tsp garlic salt.
-Celery salt and mixed herbs as required (and you **will** require them).
-2 tablespoons of chutney (Sharwood's Green Label will

do the trick nicely; however, if you have it, *'Totally French Mazaudet chutney'* is better still).
-2 thoroughly beaten eggs (when they resemble the French Rugby Team, then they are beaten enough).

Optional:
-I litre of full fresh double cream.
-1 carton of Crème Fraiche.
-1lb of Lurpak Butter.

Sensible note of interest:
Before you ask, the following abbreviations apply:

tsp	teaspoon
tbs	tablespoon
dsp	desert spoon
oz	ounce
lb	pound weight
st	stone (although I do not think there are any)
ltr*	litre
cltr*	centilitre
mltr*	millilitre
kilo*	kilogramme (kg)
km*	kilometre
gm*	gram
mgm*	film distributer

*Note: these are not really proper weights, but a sop to international relations.

What you may need besides

Some favoured friends or neighbours.
A set of correctly balanced weighing scales (what's the point of keeping unbalanced ones?)

Method

-Take the beef of some kind and cut it into smallish pieces; after which, sit aside to restore.
-When you are fully refreshed, fry the two large Spanish speaking onions in a saucepan and don't take no for an answer. (I am not going to presume to tell you how to do this. You are an adult now so work it out for yourself!*
-Add the restored meat, tomatoes, carrots (simply incised) and the large cut apple.
-Add **a** piece of bacon, if you fancy it (you choose).
-Add the 'Sauce', bring to the boil and cook slowly for about three hours, (or 180 minutes if you want to be that precise).
-At this point stir in the optional extras, but do not bring to the boil - take the boil to them.

* Note for youngsters – chop em!

Once you have completed all of the above, give yourself a pat on the back and invite favoured friends in to share the repast.

They will be impressed and your reputation as a French Chef will be made.

-o0o-

Recipe Four

TOTALLY FRENCH MAZAUDET CHUTNEY

Description

When you taste 'Total French Mazaudet Chutney' you might sense a slightly stunted rhubarb nose-growth to it, though it will lie easy on the palate. It goes very well with *Bouef au Nindel* and, as you can see, is extremely French.

Ingredients

-2kg French tomatoes.
-1kg French apples.
-A half kg of French onions.
-A selection of sultanas and raisins. (French, of course – would they use anyone else's?)
-A selection of stoned French prunes (not drunk or drugged).
-2kg of either French marrow, squash or pumpkin.
-French courgettes or aubergines (some).
-1lb French brown sugar.
-1ltr of French white wine vinegar.
-French Cider by the mugful (to be added as shown and consumed as required).
-2tsp French chilli flakes.
-About half that of Normandy sea-salt.

-A pint of French water.
-Some Angostura bitters.
Employ a French spicy bag ...that is one containing a few blades of French mace, French cardamom, French coriander, French peppercorns and French ginger.

Important notes

1. Sea-salt: ensure that the best Normandy sea-salt is used but take care to make certain that it is from well within the National-maritime-boundary or else it may become tainted by English territorial waters. It is best to use brine from an incoming tide, thus avoiding any Dover-strait's contaminant.

2. Fruit, spice and vegetable content:
Anything originating from Algeria is OK to use. Historically this used to be part of France as a whole and so counts as being, in the strict terms of this recipe, 'Totally French'. When navigating the Arc de Triomphe in Paris, you may still hear taxi-drivers sounding their horns at recalcitrant tourists with the distinctive, *"Bip-bip-bip-beep-beep!!"* sound that insists that – *"Algerie (est) Francaise!!"* – although this is becoming less common now-a-days.

What you will need besides

-A Huge French pan.
-Several pints of French beer.

-A Vietnamese alarm clock (it used to be French Indo China).
-If you're not French, a Multi-lingual dictionary.

Method

Place into the huge French pan the following:
-2kg of (French) tomatoes (skinned and roughly chopped French style - the rougher the better).
-1kg of French apples (all chopped up after removing the core and stalk – leave the skin on, it's good for you and very French into the bargain; also you feel that you are getting more your money).
-The half a kilo of French onions (similarly treated) and a good selection of French sultanas, French raisins and (possibly) un-inebriated French prunes-without-stones.
-A couple of French kilograms of either marrow, squash, pumpkin, courgettes or aubergines that you have grown in your garden if you live in France (with the skin removed - or you will be sorry!)
-The pound of brown sugar. Yes, French again.
-The pint and a half of French white wine vinegar and cider mixed together.
-Two spoons of French chilli flakes and about half that of salt.
-Then add the pint of French water and some Angostura Bitters.
-Introduce the French spicy bag to the above.
-Stoke up the French range with French logs and settle it down to a long French heating.

Cook the whole lot slowly for about 13 hours, until it all becomes gloppy.

Notes; Sit comfortably in front of your French windows with a view over the French countryside. Drink the French beer and set the French-Indo-Chinese alarm clock for 12 hours, in case you don't wake up on time.
Have a wash and brush up before putting the hot glop into suitably hot French sterilized jars and keep until Christmas.

Total French Mazaudet Chutney goes wonderfully with all kinds of French foods and makes brilliant New Year's Day presents for those of your mates to whom you forgot to send Christmas presents.

Q. What makes this recipe outrageous enough to be included in this book?
A. That you trusted all the hard work you just put in to it to the reliability of a simple F-I-C alarm clock.

Au-revoir

-oOo-

Recipe Five

GLENFARG PUDDING

Description

A most un-French, pressure-cooker recipe; and far too good to share with dogs.

We make no apology what so ever for including this very sound and original recipe in this book. It is really so splendid and of such rarity that we feel it should be shared by the World. That includes the French; and again, the French have the flair to make a good fist of it.
It comes from *'Fare and Physic of a Past Century'* sold in 1900 for the price of 2/6d* in aid of *Lady Lansdowne's Boer War Fund.* Isn't that nice?
Yes, it is!

*Twenty five pence in *'today's money'* but, in reality, it would cost you £20 to buy the book today. They were a patriotic lot back then.

Ingredients and method (as described)

"Weigh whatever the number of eggs which are necessary for the size of the pudding and add the same weight of

sugar, flour and fresh butter. When well mixed, flavour according to taste. Put into a covered mould, and steam as long as necessary."

Note
That is all it said.
It took a bit of contemplation but resulted in a beautifully light and quite delicious desert.

Here, to save you the brain-tease, are some helpful hints:
-Mix well together 3oz each of eggs, flour, butter, sugar and marmalade.
-Place in a heavily greased 'mould' (a light metal sphere in which to cook puddings) and cook in a pressure cooker at 15lbs pressure for four minutes per control-ounce of ingredients; that is:
2oz - 1hr (an anomaly)
3oz - 1hr,
4oz - 1hr 20mins.

You will need about two pints of water in the pressure-cooker and will need to reduce the pressure slowly before opening, or else the content will turn into a cannonball.

Serve with fresh cream; and, for that Christmas effect, add Mincemeat in place of Marmalade to make for yourself, a 'Lite' Xmas Pud.

I cannot emphasize strongly enough just how wonderfully delicious this dessert is. You will not find anything like it today – no matter how many Michelin Stars your local Chef has.

-o0o-

Recipe Six

BERNIE'S UNCOMPLICATED PANCAKES

Description

There are pancakes and there are Uncomplicated Pancakes; there is a difference between the two.
Being billed as an' uncomplicated' recipe you will not be surprised to learn that no complications are to be expected. However, that does not excuse you from remaining on your toes.

Ingredients:

-4oz white flour
-A pinch of salt
-An egg and a half-pint of milk (I think that roughly translates into I egg and half a pint of milk)
-Some melted butter
-Sugar to taste
-Lemon juice, orange juice, molasses, sweet chutney, lychee, Black Country yam-yams, treacle, syrup of/or fig jam (whatever suits your mood swings.)

Method:

Whisk together four ounces of flour, the pinch of salt, the egg and the half-pint of milk.

Cook it in the melted butter and, on completion, add any or all of the sugar and lemon juice or orange juice or syrup et al.
Fabulous!

What?! Oh, come on! I never said it would be complicated – coz it ain't. Just do it! K?

Useful hints:
For the ultimate pancake eating experience, open a bottle of at least three-year old, chilled Jerez Blanco Semi Dulce; draw a chair up to the fire; close the door or tent-flap, put on a record of Edith Piaf singing *'Non je ne regret rien'*; drink, eat and be merry. Students should just stick to light beer, spliffs and 'One Direction'. OAPs' use Ribena and Mario Lanza.

-o0o-

Recipe Seven

MAZAUDET COTTAGE PIE

Description

At Mazaudet, we actually make this in a Cottage. It is the original building of the hamlet (from way, way back) and about the size of a very small room; but it has a good (also very old) wood-fired 'range' in it.

Interestingly, this small building used to be the bake-house for the hamlet-ette (that's a very small 'hamlet') of Mazaudet and is equipped with, and indeed built onto, a large bread-oven – with its own brick chimney. It has since been equipped it with the 120 year old, wood-fired 'cuisiniere' that discharges into the other, smaller, brick chimney that the cottage sports. All very fascinating, particularly when considering that an ancient 'groat' was found among the cobbles when this last was being installed.

The recipe of course is easy.

For the ingredients go to Recipe One and make 'A Good Beef Stew'.

But, and here is the smart part, put the lump of meat into the pot **in a lump**, instead of **in chunks** - if you see what I mean; if you don't, then sidestep this recipe altogether.

If you do, then you will have to cook it for an extra hour; so make sure that you stoke up the range fire-box sufficiently.

What you will need besides

-A Number Two - pressure cooker, that is.

Method

-When you have finished cooking the meat, allow it to grow cold and process it through a mincer, if you can find one in this day and age.
If you can't, then you have the basis for 'Boiled Beef and Cabbage'. However, a diligent tour of the local 'vide greniere' ['*empty attic*'] market [the French version of a 'car-boot sale' – they just don't take things so far] will soon rectify that deficit. To take it a stage further, any self-respecting Rural French town that has a weekly market will likely have a stall that sells mincers and other obscure kitchen appliances (non-electric) – such as hand-wound apple peeler/corer/slicer machines. Keep looking until you find that for which you are searching [your actual, proper English].

-Once the mincing is complete, return the result to the excellent jollop that remains in the pot.
-Into your No. 2 pressure cooker, put a few potatoes and cook them in accordance with the instruction book. If you have lost this, you will just have to 'wing it.'*

-Mash the spuds up, butter 'em (adding cream, pepper and salt) and spread the resulting mess over the 'stew' – which has, by this time, been shifted to a casserole dish.

-Pop it in the oven and serve it piping hot! [Thanks are due to Benny Hill for this piece of advice.]

Useful Hint: I like to put grated cheese on top. Do you?

* 'Wing it' – choose one of the following:
-Try to remember as best you can.
-Use what is left of your imagination.
-Call a friend.
-Scrub round it altogether and settle for chips.

Bon Appetite!

-o0o-

Recipe Eight

MAZAUDET MUSHROOM OMELETTE

Description:

Well, it's a bit like a mushroom Omelette; not that exciting, but still very French!

Ingredients

-The exact amount of home-grown mushrooms that you need. These can either be 'cellar-mushrooms' or the more populous 'wild mushrooms' that grow in the Parc and surrounding fields.
-4 of Madam Gulliot's eggs (the Wise Woman of Mazaudet).
-Slat and Poivre (still French, notice).
-25cm butter.

Method

-First, enter your cellar and pick your ration of mushrooms; or walk round the Parc and pick your mushrooms from there. Cut with a sharp knife, taking care not to pull the roots out of the floor, or you will find you have none next time you want mushrooms.
-Then, go next-door and plead for four eggs from Madame Guillot. (In French - she speaks nothing else, except Portuguese – which you probably don't.)

-Cook the mushrooms in butter with some slat and poivre.
-Heat some more butter in a pan (frying) until almost
actually smoking.   -Pour in the
eggs - which you had previously whisked up with some
pepper and chopped chives. Did I forget to tell you to
provide these extras? How forgetful of me. Not to worry,
you know now.
-Cook briefly.
-Put the mushrooms in the centre, fold the two outside
edges inwards to cover the 'shrooms and serve it to
someone you like.

In return, they will surely like you back.

Recipe Nine

GOOD DOG FOOD

Explanation

Some of you may be both shocked and surprised in equal measure to see a recipe wholly for dogs in a quality publication, such as this. Well! I have it on fairly good authority (see recipe one) that, in rural France, dogs sometimes, no - make that always, mess with their masters and/or mistresses. So here goes - a recipe for 'Good Dog Food'

Question: (what do 'Bad Dogs' eat in France, I wonder?)

Ingredients and method
-Put any meat, two carrots and a pint of stock into the low-pressure cooker, bring to that pressure and simmer for one hour.
-Cool and serve with a biscuit or bone garnish.

Dogs love it.

(Otherwise feed them the left-overs from 'A Good Beef Stew'. It's still better than that which a lot of students eat in Britain.)

-o0o-

Recipe Ten (alpha)

'PER-PERSON' PORK POT (PPPP)

Description

This cheap old country farmhouse recipe (and you may read that in any of many ways) is much loved in rural France. It keeps the inhabitants warm in winter, gives them plenty of belly ballast for mucking out the chicken coup or pig sty and the taste lingers until well after the RTE 9pm watershed.

It is quite easy to make; does not require much room; is fairly inexpensive; is definitely cholesterol inducing and, depending upon how tight/loose you are with the goose-grease, will normally give you an undisturbed night.

Ingredients

-A Cheap Pork Piece – in season.
-Butter and goose fat.
-Potatoes and carrots.
-Apples and onions.
-Cider and flour.
-Salt'n'pepper.
-Angostura Bitters (no one knows why).

Note; Ingredient quantities are accountably missing owing to bad reception on radio 'All Algerie' (108mghz on the

Ocean Wave) but for 'starters' use half of what you think you will need - and for 'the main course' use double.

Method

-Go buy a quantity of cheap pork – in some parts of the year it is even cheaper.
-Cut off the bone and shape it (the meat) into cubes, triangles or rhomboids as you wish.
-Place the bone into a large casserole pot and add a certain quantity of Angostura Bitters.
-Place a generous amount of butter and goose-grease in a frying-pan and add the diced amount of apples and onions (the latter to be salt-and-peppered) as follows: one each per person to be fed (hence the name of the dish).
-Fry until soft, when you will extract the solids and add them to the casserole dish, leaving behind the nutritious jollop.
-Roll the pork-meat in salt-n-pepper'd flour before putting most of it, OK, all of it, into the frying-pan jollop.
-Seal the meat over a high heat (2 meters or more gives the best results).

Note: you may have to add more handfuls of goose-grease, but the 'why' was lost in translation.

-Pour the whole content from the frying-pan into the casserole dish, adding two cloves per person.*
-Meanwhile you should have diced carrots and potatoes in similar quantities and put them into the pot also. If you

didn't, then a black mark will be put against your name and you should carry on as normal. (These things just happen.)
-Finally, add a third of a pint of cider (in fluid ounces) and a third of a pint of chicken stock (in centilitres) - again, per person - put on the lid and cook slowly for several hours.

When all is deemed to be ready, invite the neighbours round for supper – particularly the Madame Guillot who gave you those eggs.

This dish may be followed, advantageously, by a good 'Glenfarg Pudding' q.v.

* Note: whoever gets the fewest cloves – does the washing-up.

-o0o-

Recipe Ten (bravo)

PPPP DUMPLINGS

If you add dumplings to the 'Per-person Pork Pot, you will be well pleased.

Take 4oz flour, 2oz suet, 5 tbspms (table-spoons?) water, parsley and herbs unspecified and squooge them up into eight dumpling-shaped balls. Roll these in flour and drop them into the PPPP half an hour before end of cooking. This is what is known in maritime circles as 'belly-timber, ah-haar!'.

-o0o-

Recipe Eleven

BURGOO!
[French style]

Description

Well! It's not a fast dish.
Equally it's not a slow dish.
Also, it's not an expensive dish.
Nor could you call it a cheap dish.
It's not a hot dish but….. it's better not eaten cold either.
Tell you what ….. cook it and surprise your children.

Ingredients

-5 carrots. Ordinary, mass-produced carrots will do
because, quite frankly, special, sandal-fed, long-haired,
Bio-carrots are much too good for Burgoo.
-5 potatoes. Old or new – it really does not matter – unless
you are trying to impress someone.
-2 Onions. Bi-lingual onions are fine for this; but avoid
Stalin-esque ones.
-Tournesoil. (The oil from the Sunflower – 'Tourne-au-
soleil' (or *turn to the sun*, as the French have it.)
-Saussise-sec; the preserved sausage of the region – much
akin to a rough type of salami.
-Poitrine, pork-belly cut into tiny, tiny little bits.
-Porridge Oats.

What you will also need

-The good old, trusty pressure-cooker.
-The standard extras – salt, pepper, herbs, stock cube, bay-leaves etc.
-The Bakelite Standard Stirring Spoon (BSSS) – available at all good Ironmongers, if you can find one of either.
-An axe.

Method

-Take five medium carrots and chunk them (we do a lot of that at Mazaudet).
-Do the same to a similar amount of potatoes.
-Also chunk the pair of onions and fry these in the bottom of the pressure-cooker (without lid or trivet) in the tournesoil.
-When the onions are soft, add the carrots and spuds and some chopped-up saussise-sec (2" of 'baton' or equivalent) or some 'poitrine' (lardons) for extra taste.

Note
This may seem a little 'foreign' to you – all this talk of 'baton' and 'lardons' – but it may give you some incentive to visit the home of Mazaudet Country Cooking to find out what it is all about.

-Put in a few pinches of sea-salt (you'll know when it's enough – believe me), ground pepper (on the same basis), a Bay leaf and some herbs (as you wish).

-Add a pint of stock-cube-stock and fit the lid.

Now, I am assuming that you are *au-fait* (that's yer actual French) with your galley-range and know just how much coal/wood/oil with which to stoke it; so will not pursue that further.

-Cook at 15lb pressure for six minutes and reduce said force by cooling in water (cold). Remove the lid and add two handfuls of porridge oats, stir with the BSSS and cook over a low heat for a few minutes (10mins, in actuality).

Dish it up and get it daahn-yer. Mmmmm!

There will be enough left over to fry for breakfast - probably because no one else likes it – which is when it will be best of all. But people are funny the way of 'not liking things'; they have the same reaction to the celebrated 'Fish'n'rice dish' (see Recipe 22); yet they are both very good to eat.

-o0o-

Recipe Twelve

BIRTHDAY PORK CHOP

Description

This the *'Lesser known 'Birthday' Pork Chop'*.
In France the *'Greater known 'Celebration' Pork Chop'* is always eaten on Easter Monday regardless of any other consideration. Why this should be so is regarded as one of the great secrets of the *'Guild of Cassoulet Chefs'* (second in influence only to *'La Chasse'*), whose secret recipes and their accompanying rituals are available only to Extra-master Cassoulerious – not us mere mortals. So unless you are lucky enough to celebrate your birthday at Easter, then this has to be for you. It could be your last chance.

Ingredients

-A single, 1 kilo Pork Chop. (Now, that is one massive pork chop and available in season all over the Limousin. If it is not enough for you – go to Cyprus where they are even bigger.)
-Four-eights of an apple.
-A squirt of Sage.
-A smother Acacia honey.
-Half a litre of 'le Cidre'.
-A couple of handfuls of goose-grease.

What you will need besides

-An enamelled self -basting roasting dish.
-An enamelled self -basting roasting dish lid ... for the use of.
-A goodly amount of booze.
-One friend to offer their congratulation and to photograph the event. (Sad, or what?)
-At least a radio, for goodness sake.

Method

-Smother the 1 kilo Pork Chop in the goose-grease and give it a good squoogie around before putting it into the self-basting roasting dish.
-Add the four-eigth'd apple and sprinkle in sage, black pepper and sea-salt.
-Smother the whole lot with Acacia honey.
-Add half a litre of 'le cidre' (or more in French) and put on the lid.
-Cook for four hours in a slow oven and, by the way -

Have a Happy Birthday!

(You only get to do this once a year; so how many more times have you got?)

-o0o-

Recipe Thirteen

BREAKFAST EYE

Description

The recipe is perfect for those looking for nothing more than an ever-so-slight challenge. You won't even need to get out of bed if you don't want to. How about that?! A breakfast you don't even have to get out of bed to cook. What ground-breaking frippery for the laziest of society's sloths this is.

Ingredients

-A melange of yesterdays mashed potato and vegetable left-overs.   -A handful of duck fat.
-A hen's egg or, for a special occasion - a duck's egg or; for that extra special occasion – a goose's egg.
-Relish (optional)

Method

Into a small frying pan (hot) put the melange of yesterday's mashed-up potatoes, vegetables etc and cook in a little duck fat until the bottom is quite crisp and the whole thing can slide around the pan without breaking up.

Make a clear space in the middle (like a lifebelt – which it certainly ain't!) into which break an egg (without rupturing the yoke).
Place a lid over the pan and cook until the egg achieves your favoured consistency.*
This is a 'Breakfast Eye' and may be slid straight from the pan onto a plate and eaten with the optional relish**.

Notes: *for 'consistency', Members of Parliament read – 'constituency'.
** I don't know where you can obtain Optional Relish, but the Maz Chef d'Cuisine would not be too upset if you decided to use Branston's or Sharwood's instead.
However, it is understood that Optional Relish is closely related to Portable Soup (see O'Brien's 'Master and Commander'.)

Recipe Fourteen
MEALY PUDDING

Description

At the almost famous 'Mazaudet Country Kitchen', the following recipe was the first of many concoctions and is about as basic as it gets; thus it is ideal for anyone on a really tight budget - or 'nearly skint', as the Mazaudetians have it. If you cannot manage to cook this then you deserve to go hungry.

So with that in mind, let's get to it:

Ingredients (optional but should include at least some of the following)
-4oz* Oatmeal
-2oz suet
-1 onion
-A kilo of marshmallows
-Seasoning (fresh winter variety only)
-Some butter (preferably Lurpak)

*Important Note:
an 'oz' is an 'ounce', which is a sixteenth part of a 'pound' (weight). This is in itself about half the weight of a 'kilogram' – which then wanders off into a realm of its own, ie: metric measure. No-one actually knows what this is all about, so we at the Mazaudet Country Kitchen prefer

to stick to 'real weights' (pounds, ounces, that sort of thing), which at least bear some resemblance to everyday life. For example: a 'pound' is as much as a baby can lift on a bench-press.

What you may need besides

A pretty fertile imagination if you fancy something else; which is why the marshmallows have been included. Use them as you see fit.
Also, as this is a 'Mazaudet pressure-cooker mealy pudding', a pressure cooker would be quite handy.

Method

Mix together 4oz of oatmeal, 2oz of suet and a chopped onion.
Season well with salt and pepper.
Tip the lot into a bag or mould and cook at high pressure (yes, in such a cooker) for twenty minutes.
[Interesting note: the Mazaudet pressure cooker is validated until 1969 but is still in daily use and appears none the worse for wear.]
Release the pressure ever so slowly.
Set aside and allow to cool and to set.

When sufficiently solid, either:
-slice and fry in butter with whatever accompaniment you might choose – as required;
-or roll into balls and fry in 'sausage-juice'.

From the Michelan Guide correspondent's notes:

"Ahhh! Therein lays the genius of the Mazaudet system. Don't you just love that final touch - 'Sausage Juice!!!'? Who else do you know would have the daring to pull such a culinary master stroke as that? Certainly none of those self-confessed celebrities who currently grace our television screens and that's a fact. Bernie has certainly breathed new life into cheap and nasty cooking."

Note: Keep a supply handy in the fridge. You never know who is going to drop in or when you are likely to become shipwrecked.

Subsidiary note: What are the Marshmallows for? To put to one side just in case the Mealy Pudding fails to make the grade. At least you will have something to offer if someone does unaccountably drop in.

-oOo-

Recipe Fifteen

TRADITIONAL CHRISTMAS PUDDING

Description

There are many recipes for Christmas Pudding and you must decide just how 'heavy' you require it to be. Probably the best of all, in regard to waist-line, is the *Glenfarg Pudding* (q.v.).
This one is medium-light and very good. It will transform your perception of the 'Trad Xmas Pud' completely.

Ingredients

You will need the following:
-1/2lb raisins,
-1/2lb suet,
-1/4lb currents,
-1/4lb brown breadcrumbs,
-2oz flour,
-2oz brown sugar,
-½ tumbler of rum,
-½ tsp salt,
-½ tsp grated nutmeg,
-A large measure of Masala,
-3 eggs,
-1/4pt milk,
-1 heaped tablespoon of black treacle (good luck!),

-The grated rind of half a lemon and its juice.

What you will need besides

-Well, of course, all the usual things that you will find in the Country Kitchen. If you do not know by now.... what hope is there?
-A sprig of holly.
-False snow (all will be revealed).

Method

-Beat the eggs and the milk together, using your Sub-prime All-purpose Beating Utensil, or 'Sabu', as it is sometimes known.
-Put on an apron and try again.
-Then mix all the other ingredients together (stand-fast the rum and the treacle) in a large, large basin.
-Once everything is mixed to your satisfaction, add the milk/eggs mix, the treacle and most of the rum and stir up well.
-Leave it for an hour before mixing again.
-Pour the measure of Masala into a nice cut-glass goblet and quaff (now, there's a word you don't see very often) as, after all, it is Christmas and you are stuck in the kitchen making all the festive cheer. Why shouldn't you have a little treat now and again?

Ah-ha! You have some rum left over? Drink that as well and feel that warm, Christmassy glow spread throughout your extremities. This is one of the *'joys of the season'*.

Meanwhile, back to the cooking:
-Bring a huge pan of water to the boil.
-Place the mixture from the basin into a suitable cloth, tie up and place in a wire basket.
-Put the wire basket et al into the boiling water and leave it there for **five hours** in a constant state of a-boilingness.

After five hours:
-Remove from the water and hang up to drain.
-Once this draining has occurred, re-hang in a cool place (the game-larder will do) until required.

Serving

-Boil (as previously indicated) for a further four hours or steam for six.
-Remove from the cloth.
-Place on a traditional serving dish, garnish with holly and that kind-of snow-like icing you see in the old pictures (how frightfully gay!), and serve with lashings of cream and rum-butter:

....................soften butter, add sugar and mix rum into it.

Note: Do not put coins into this pudding. Dentists (if you can find one over the Holidays) are very expensive.

Bonne Noel!

-o0o-

Recipe Sixteen

'DEAD RABBIT'

Description

Once upon a time there was a Rabbit who happened to be looking the wrong way when Maria came to give him his daily cuddle.
This is the result and let it be a warning to all other rabbits.

Here's what Maria told me to do (in French. I have translated it).

"Put the (two halves) into the pot with a little thyme, some lemon, a little thyme, Bay-leaves, much parsley, onions, carrots, more thyme, a little garlic, chicken stock and lots of fine-ground black pepper.
Pressure cook at 15lbs for 20 minutes and cool the pressure slowly."

"Make a roux sauce with butter and flour; strain all the juices from the pot and add to the roux to make the sauce. Simmer to reduce to 2/3 the original amount. Add a healthy dollop of that (points to 'Moutard de Limousin') and put to one side."

She then tore the flesh off the carcass, scattered it atop a pile of pure'd potatoes and covered with the sauce.

My! But it was good!
Thank you Madame Maria.

-o0o-

Recipe Seventeen

SCHNAPPFULWERKENKAIKE

[Possibly from Germany]

Description

This is a very typical North German recipe, full of hearty but simple ingredients. As you would expect from any North Rhine-Westphalia dish, it is extremely strong, robust, rust-resistant; full of very strong, hearty, irony-green vegetable-like ingredients and built to last - with oodles of add-ons and technical innovations to improve the flavours; but beware of the post eating exhaust emissions.They could be over the proscribed US limits for such things.

Schnappfulwerkenkaike* is made by millions (well hundreds at least) of German working class housewives on a daily basis. They pause just long enough for it to be 'cool' then pack it into their husbands' lunchboxes to take to the Volksworks, before continuing with their busy but mundane lives.

*This makes a good breakfast dish and will set you up for a day's hard labour in the Volksworks communal 'werkhause'.

Ingredients

-1portion of three-day-old, cooked, white cabbage.
-Left-over mashed potato from the last time it was on your menu.
-2 Oldenburg eggs.
-Chives, parsley, salt and pepper.
-Goose grease (a technical upgrade from lard) or axle-grease to obtain that authentic, Westphalian workers' tang.

Method

Take the three-day-old, cooked white cabbage and the mashed potato found lurking in the back of the fridge ('Smeg' of course) and either mix or blend it with a couple of eggs.
Add chives, pepper, parsley and salt and fry a whole lot in geese-grease or axle-grease as desired.

Before issuing to any third party, read them this important safety warning;

Important Safety Warning!

'Schnappfulwerkenkaike' consumers should be allowed clear and unobstructed access to the Volksworks ablutions block for at least one shift after clocking out.
You can get your free pass from the works' Tikketstumbumfuhrer.

-o0o-

Recipe Eighteen

LAST NIGHT's PASTA SAUCE PLUS

Description

As with all Mazadetian recipes, if you need a description then this recipe is probably one step too far, too soon. Go back to Recipe One and collect a food voucher as you pass the Cottage Bake-house.

The recipe got its name through simply referencing its ingredients. There was not much leeway for calling it anything but, except that *'anything but'* would not be a suitable title as it excludes the *'plus'*. ('But, but, but' – these are spare 'but's in case you run short of 'but's or are a fan of BSA Bantam motorcycles.)

Ingredients

-Yesterday's Pasta Sauce ('cos that's what it's called) plus a few little extras to bulk it out.
-Pasta.
-Boiling water.
-A small olive oil.

Method
-Saute' (cook very slowly while chucking it about a bit, on a low heat, in goose-grease - as in other Mazaudetian recipes) the few little extras you have decided to

incorporate. These could include chopped garlic and onion, for example, or if you can stretch a little further this week, an aubergine and mushroom melange.

-*However, don't do that yet. First of all, wash an aubergine, chop it and cover with a sprinkling of salt.*

-Leave it for a bit - while you do that thing that you have left undone but ought to have done - thus, perhaps, averting disaster..

-When you have finished, squeeze it, drain it and put-it-aside.

-Slice some peppers and any mushrooms, if you have them.

-Chop parsley, rosemary and basil.

-Now you can get on with the onion/garlic bit *(see above)*.

-After all that, you should add the aubergine, peppers, mushrooms and, if you have them, a parsmarybaaz'l mixture –oh! - and the red/white wine.

(Sorry, I should have mentioned that before. It is always a good idea to have some wine available in the kitchen. Drink some; put some in the preparation; offer a glass or two to your dogs. You will find them very interested in what you are doing.)

Note This recipe is for 'when you are on your own' but that's not much fun, is it? Always better to have friends around – if only to share the wine. So go get on the phone.

Where were we up to? Oh yes.

-Leave the concoction to simmer for half an hour while you....

-Choose your pasta – normally the one that looks like a bird's nest – and put it into the boiling water, leaving it there for about five minutes.

-Once it is cooked (and have no truck with the 'throwing it against the wall to see if it sticks' school of cuisinery; which is about as futile as inverting a bowl of whisked egg-whites above your head to see if they are properly stiff), add the small olive oil (or a little olive oil) into the pasta, stir and then dump the whole lot into the sauce – which has been deemed, by you (and you have to take responsibility for these things) to be ready.

-Leave it to sit quietly for two minutes, then garnish with Parmesan chiz (grated) and season as usual with usual seasoning, in season – usually.

And that's it.

Why 'Last Night's Pasta Sauce'? Well. If you are not so almightyly tight-fisted as to make merely enough, there is normally some of it left over - which can be excellently re-heated for your breakfast.

-o0o-

Recipe Nineteen

MAZAUDET 'FRIDGE-CULL' TART

Description

This originates from a 'clear-out' that occurred on thirteenth of November in 2007, and remains valid to this day.

Let's see what we have in the refrigerator and think what we can do with it, for you will all have these sorts of things, for sure. They seem to lurk round the back of the beer cans until they are way past their use-by dates. No problem there; those dates are artificial in any case and only apply to the wealthy and those with little common sense. (Could be one and the same – you never can tell.) Use your well-honed senses, particularly your nose, as a guideline, instead of the manufacturers' labels. However, it is a little more difficult to do this when assessing *"....glacial-spring mountain water, filtered through rock for 3,000 years – use before next Tuesday."*

Found ingredients

Say:

-An onion

-Some garlic

-Various types of lubricant (except automotive)

-Any old bacon, or similar substances (but not **too** smelly)

-Brown sugar

-Seasoning (if you keep it there)
-Two old tomatoes
-Old pieces of pastry that may be tucked away somewhere out of sight and any cheese that moulders next to it. (Old, mouldy cheese is 'ace' for proper cuisine cooking.)

Method

-Chop up two onions and some garlic, season with salt and pepper and fry in goose grease or duck fat or, if health conscious, sunflower oil, until they are soft but not brown.

Note: this is the standard commencement point for most cooking (particularly when in France) and so it is in the Mazaudet Country Kitchen.

-Chop up four bacon slices or something vaguely similar and augment with any remaining smoked Lardons that you have remaining from previous culinary adventures.
-Add these to the onions, with two teaspoons of brown sugar. Don't cook any more. (Not in quantity, that is, but in time.)
-Chop up the two tomatoes, after seasoning with the usual slat, popper, shugar and Baazil. (Note the spellings used there. Uniquely only the Mazaudet Country Kitchen spells in this way.)
-Leave to one side just for the moment.
-Cool it.

-Roll out that piece of pastry that seems to have been lurking in the back shelf for a decade and slap it into a shallow dish with a loud 'Shlaaap!'

-Now, (having pre-heated the oven) you would normally cook the pastry 'blind' for a while, although you will still be able to see it. Baking blind means covering the bottom part of the pastry with some of your old marbles, or some similar clay looking thingy's, so as to keep the bottom from rising. In this case, you don't have to – because Mazaudetians have a 'wheeze'; also, as all the cooking is being done by a one hundred year old 'Cuisiniere'*, powered by wood. So, here is the 'wheeze':

"Arrange the tomato, onion, et al on the pastry in a pleasing pattern and cook in the oven for about fifteen minutes - if not very hot; or seven minutes - if very hot. It all depends on how much wood you are prepared to squander and how much 'draught' you arrange. This in turn is dependent upon the ambient temperature of the house which, as the 'Cuisiniere' is also the main form of heating, can fluctuate with the weather. It all seems a bit complicated but, once you are living in a 'last century' environment (or even the one before that!), it all becomes really quite easy; any students amongst you may well be doing just that, anyway."

* 'Cuisieiere' – wood-fired cooking stove. The stove in the Mazaudet Country Kitchen is actually a coal-fired cooking stove that burns wood (we can't get the coal in this part of the world, you see), which makes cooking - or in this case

'Cuisiniere cooking' - a little more complicated and therefore much more interesting.

-Once the pastry has been cooked, pour on six Bantam eggs (well beaten) and sprinkle in/on the grated left-overs of all the cheese that has been lurking next to the pastry. Shut the oven right down (I won't describe how this is done as, if you do not have a 100yr old Cuisiniere designed for coal [unobtainable in rural France] but powered by wood [which grows all around], there is very little point) and bake the tart for an hour – or however long seems appropriate with the appliance you are using.
-*Why bantams eggs?'* you may ask. Well, there are no secrets here. Simply because they were the only hens belonging to the Mazaudet Country Kitchen and, at the time of this recipe's discovery, they were laying well. Since then, with aquatic foul in the ascendancy, duck-eggs have become the norm. Anyway – they are better for you.

Useful tip
-Make sure that you turn the tart round at the half-way point to allow even cooking and to prevent burning on the fire-box side of the oven.

There now; that was not too difficult, was it? And the great thing about it is, you got yourself a clean fridge ready to collect more 'mundungus' (ask any Naval pal) for the next 'Fridge Cull'

HealthWarning

Don't use anything that is: green and powdery;
uncommonly sticky; opaquely slimy to the touch;
generally rusty; has a white fur coat growing on it; is too
limp to be revived in cold water or too crusty to break with
an ordinary-sized kitchen mallet.

-o0o-

Recipe Twenty

MOTHER BRUEN'S VERY BEST TOMATO SANDWICHES

Description

The best thing about this recipe is that it gives the reader access to the finest tomato sandwiches in the world. Once tasted, you will never want any other kind – unless, of course it be one of Mother Bruen's Celebrated Egg Sandwiches (of which more anon).

Ingredients

-Freshly sliced white or brown bread
-Soft butter
-Tomatoes
-Fresh parsley
-Fresh bazil
-Seasoning to taste
-Angostura Bitters

What you will need besides

-All the usual kitchen implements

Method

-Cut two reasonably thick slices of bread and butter them liberally.

-Skin the tomatoes by dipping in boiling water, dipping in cold water and picking off the skin. This is the difficult part.

-Now slice them, discard all the pips and the juice and place the slices on a chopping board.

-Chop up the flesh in a fine way and add parsley/bazil (also chopped).

-Season with salt and pepper and (this is the key!) *a little sugar*.

-Add a few drops of Angostura Bitters.

-Mix the whole lot together and spread on the bread, adding a slice on top to make a sandwich.

-Remove the crusts (this is important), cut into four (diagonally, also important) and serve with a garnish of parsley.

You will not believe just how good this is. The finest Tomato Sandwiches in the world.

In order to make Mother Bruen's Celebrated Egg Sandwiches...

You will need to hard-boil some eggs (hens' are best but free-range are even better). Allow them to become cool.

-When they are thus rendered un-hot, peel off the shells and chop the residue (white and yoke) into a coarse, yet refined, consistency.

-Add to this some mayonnaise - which you may either make yourself (best) or get from a jar (un-best). Should you wish to make the mayonnaise yourself, which is a difficult thing to do and well beyond the scope of this book, find a copy of the Good Housekeeping Cook Book (circa 1945) and follow the directions within. Old Mother Bruen did this as a young bride and never looked back. So, if it was good enough for her......

-Also add some finely chopped chives and a little white pepper.

-Now, mix the whole lot together and spread thickly on previously buttered white bread.

-Very lightly dust with Cayenne pepper and do the sandwich trick of putting on the 'lid' of bread.

-Remove the crusts. Cut into quarters (square or diagonal – it doesn't matter this time), garnish with a parsley sprig and serve on a pretty, porcelain plate.

It is doubtful whether anyone will be able to state a preference between these two totally spiffing tea-time treats and you will have gained a reputation for provision of the most 'sandwichiest' sandwiches on the planet.

Well done!

-o0o-

Recipe Twenty-one

SUGARLESS MARMALADE

A Bonus Recipe

Description

There are control-freaks on my television every day of the week banging on about the amount of sugar we are all consuming. You can't even take a mouthful of your favourite breakfast 'jam doughnut' without being made to feel guilty and inferior. So it behoves the Mazaudet Country Cookhouse to enter the ring and declare what we should be doing for the overly-sugared population of these long suffering countries of ours.

It is easy to make and, without the added sugar, costs less.

What you will need:

-Six large Seville Oranges
-Three medium sized lemons
-1.5 litres of fresh, un-chlorinated water.

Then as the late Jimmy Young used to say daily, *"This is what you do."*

-First peel the oranges and lemons; cut the peel into small slices (or your favourite shapes – just to add variety) and place in a large boiling-pan.

-Squeeze the hell out of the 'Bells of St Clements'* until they are all relieved of their juices, and pour said juice on top of the peel.

-Cutting the remainder of the fruit into quarters, place it into a muslin, repeat - 'muslin', cloth which you put in the pan with the top tied off to the pan-handle. Now, that's quite simple, isn't it?

-Instead of adding sugar (note: this is a sugarless recipe), add the 1.5litres of water, place the pan onto a heat-source and bring the contents to the boil; continuing for as long as it takes to reduce the water by half.

-Then, using some method as devised by yourself (No, we are not going to tell you. Where's the fun in that?), squeeze the hot muslin bag strongly, to extract all of the goodness from within it.

-While the water is reducing, preheat and sterilize several empty jars

* 'Bells of St Clements' – nearly rhyming slang for 'oranges and lemons' – or vice versa, perhaps.

Note: at this point, if you had included sugar to the recipe, you would test it to see if the mix was setting. You would do this by taking a small amount of the 'jam' and placing it on a plate in a cool location and seeing if it solidified; but as we are making a sugarless marmalade, we will skip that part - as it will only take up your valuable sleeping/browsing/sailing time. But do feel free to add a half bottle of whisky if you like.

-Fill the empty pots with the hot marmalade and seal them.
-Place the filled jars in a cool place (but not the sort of 'cool' that your kids understand, mind) until needed.
-Label each jar clearly – *'Dipping Marmalade'*. That will confuse the sceptics.

A warning note: when you come to use your sugarless marmalade, remember that it will not be stiff or jellified like the heavily sugared shop bought variety; so be careful how you spread it. We recommend using a spoon to scoop it onto the toast and use the butter to build a low wall around the edge of the bread to contain it. Also, keep a steady hand as you take the toast from plate to face, or you will end up with something reminiscent of a Singapore Marmalade Banjo.
We never said it there would not be problems, but at least it does not have any added sugar.

Mmmm! good for you and delicious in one.

Subsidiary notes:
1.   An alternative to spreading the marmalade on the toast is to take a bite of the buttered toast, swiftly followed by a spoon-full of the confectionary. Then chew the whole lot up together.
2.   If the 'whole lot' is rather too 'tart' for your taste, add a spoon-full of sugar. I won't tell anyone if you don't.

-o0o-

Recipe Twenty-two

EAST OF SUEZ FISH CURRY
[otherwise known as *'Samik wa riz'* or, simply the more infamous *'Fish'n'Rice'*]

Description

The recipe was 'cooked-up' by the culinary genius of the Mazaudet Country Kitchen even before it had come into existence. It was created to be eaten in a yacht sailing from the Middle East, around the Cape of Storms (Good Hope) and back to England-land. It uses little water and less fuel and one never gets bored of/with/from it.

Also it has a definitive Middle Eastern flavour which, had you been there, would transport you back to the road-side 'finger-dip restaurant' at Wudam-on-the-Mud (Oman) where you first tasted it. So it is a kind-of magic carpet ride for the memory – but in reverse.

The beauty of this, like all Mazaudet dishes, is that it is so unrelentingly simple.

What you will need:

-A can of 'in date' tinned fish (mackerel, sardines, herring or pilchards).
-One piece of onion a-piece.
-Curry powder to taste.
-A cup of plain rice (each).
-Some butter (or ghee – in a tin).

-Some more butter/ghee.

What you do with it:

-Boil the rice until it is done. The easiest way to do this is to combine the rice and the water and boil it until the latter has disappeared; making sure to remove from the heat before the rice starts to stick to the bottom and burn (or you will also need a good quantity of extra quality Wire Wool).
-Meanwhile, chop and fry the onion piece(s) with a generous amount of the curry powder. Use some of the butter to do this.
-Add to this a tin of whatever fish you managed to get your hands on and continue to cook until the fish is a crispy colour (whatever colour that should be depends upon the fish you chose).
-Butter the rice and add the fish and there you have it. Simple

Money saving tip: Fry-up the left-overs for the next day's breakfast.
That is the hallmark of Mazaudet cooking - money saving versatility.

Effort saving tip - and this will save time, fuel and the use of the second pan:
When the rice is cooked, add to it the fish, ghee and curry powder, and continue to cook for a few minutes. Eat it out of the pan – this saves on washing-up.

Food saving tip: Keep the onion for another day.

Face saving tip: Don't offer it to anyone else as it has become traditional *'....not to like it.'* Keep it just for you – and the Dogs.

-o0o-

Recipe Twenty-three

OMANI FORMULA ONE CURRY

Description

The ingredients and method sections have been combined in order to save you time before the race gets underway.

Part one:
-Into a pressure cooker put a large lump of meat - belly pork (not easy to come by in Bahrain), shin'o'beef, neck'o'lamb, head of goat or such like - two onions and some potatoes.
-Add salt, some herbs from the garden and a pint of water.
-Cook at low pressure for about half an hour; after which you can remove any bones, fat, skin or eyes (if you used them), or add some as you wish.
-Place any unwanted bones in the ready-use basin ready for the dogs. (Note: you really must empty this soon.)

Part two:
-In a large frying pan cook another couple of onions, with as much curry powder as you deem acceptable and a few cumin seeds.
-Now add the meat, potatoes and other onions from the pressure cooker, having chopped them up into bits.
-Cook it all up with some milk/cream/yoghurt to make a creamy sauce.
-Take it off the cooker.

-After a little time, serve it up as brown bread sandwiches for you and your mates.

These sandwiches are delicious and relatively easy to eat. Have some more.

Then for the *'piece of resistance'*;
Open a bottle of Champagne and settle down to watch the F1 Grand Prix on the TV and, afterwards or (more likely) during, – fall asleep.
Alternatively, go and play badminton in the swimming pool.

-oOo-

Recipe Twenty-four

TOMATO SOUPE

Description
You will notice that, here, the format changes somewhat.
Well, we have been together now for many pages and so
perhaps we know each other well enough to be a little
more – shall we say – colloquial.
So, as the man with the big hat said,
"Time for a change, anyway."

What you should do
-First of all, chop two onions into teeny-weeny pieces and
then do likewise with two cloves of garlic.
-Fry the result in duck-fat (it makes a change from the
usual goose-grease and is better for you), along with some
Lardons (smoked are best), until the vegetable matter is
soft but not brown.
-Now add the content of a tin of tomatoes.

Useful tip: before taking the toms out of the tin, shuggle
them about with a sharp knife* and they will come out all
chopped up. Alternatively, you could always buy tinned
'pre-chopped' tomatoes.

-Also pour in some chicken stock (if you have made some;
if not, a stock-cube and hot water will pass at a pinch),
season with salt and pepper (a pinch each) and garnish
with Baazil.

-A little Lee and Perrin's Worcestershire Sauce will add piquancy and some Angostura Bitters will give that ethereally elusive flavour that will have your clients (clients? Who are you?) wanting more.
-Simmer gently for twenty three minutes, wiz-up with the wizzy-machine, adjust seasoning to taste and serve.

To be frightfully *'novelle cuisine'*, swirl in some cream in a delightful swirly shape and dust with chopped Baazil. Mmmm – yummie!

* **Sharp knife**. Despite what your Nanny might have told you, knives should always be sharp, otherwise they are just metal sticks and you may as well use a drinking-straw.

-o0o-

Recipe Twenty-five

A WARMING PIG STEW

Description (or not)

It's all here, down below; because sometimes it is more interesting to read a recipe as a piece of prose instead of as a recipe. That's how *Glenfarg Pudding* did it and, as an admirer of *Glenfarg Pudding*, that's the way I am going to do it for a bit. [So sayeth the Mazaudet chef – if somewhat archaically.]

-Take an upper-arm of Pig and cook in a pressure-cooker (with two pints of water) for an hour or so.
-Use a low pressure and all will be well.
-Once this process has been completed, remove the bones and place them in the ready-use dog-basin.
-Give the rind and the fat to the dogs – who will be absolutely delighted and will show their appreciation by jumping up and down. Billy Apricot* (the poodle) may even do a little dance – it is what he does.
-Add the following to the remaining meat:
diced potatoes, diced carrots, diced celery, diced onions and sliced chorizo; garlic, black pepper, some salt, red wine, cloves, mushrooms, red/white beanz, a large tot of Vermouth (*the secret ingredient*) and some flour cooked in grease-goose.

Note: having progressed thus far you should have a pretty good handle on how much of what to add to the various concoctions here displayed. So just get on with it. K?

-Put the pan (pressure cooker without the pressure lid) on a trivet over a low heat, with an ordinary lid on it (or the pressure lid without the valve closed – easier) and leave for an hour or two.
-Let it cool and put to one side.
-When you feel hungry, take some out, heat it up and have a feast. It really is jolly good!   * [In an alternative universe – *Billy Apricot and the Soft Fruit Boys.*]

-o0o-

Recipe Twenty-six
A SIMPLE PIG CASSEROLE
Not to be confused with a 'Cassoulet'

This is very much like Recipe Twenty-five - except that it is a bit different.

-Take the other upper-arm of Pig and cook under pressure for an hour – much as you did in R-25.
-Whilst you are waiting, take a good, cast-iron casserole (or 'Marmite', as they have it in France – and they do) and place into it the following bitz and piecez:

> one tin of red lentils (discard the tin),
> three medium potatoes (or equivalent) - chopped,
> several cloves of garlic,
> any frozen peas that are lurking in the freezer-chest,
> one large onion (partially fried),
> some herbs of choice,
> pepper and salt and - -

A thickening sauce:
-cook together a tablespoon each of flour, duck-grease and honey.

Note: you can do this first if you like, in the Marmite, before adding the above; it is all a matter of choice, of which there are many at Mazaudet.

-When the Pig is cooked, remove the bones to the ready-use basin and, as before, give the rind and fat to the lucky, lucky dogs (dance, Billy, dance!).

-Making a stock of the remaining juices (by adding a bouillon cube of either chicken or vegetable stuff), place the meat in the casserole or the Marmite.

-Place the Marmite on the top of the stove (on a trivet) and allow to cook for – oh – I don't know.... a long time – 'til it's done.

I am sure it will be very good, especially on a cold, wet, rainy, winter's day like it is today.

Final note: You will have a bowl full of left-over bones by now. What to do with them?

Bury them in odd places around the Demesne as a delightful treasure-hunt for Billy Apricot and his friends. They will love you all the more for it.

-o0o-

Recipe Twenty-seven

SOUPE DE BIÈRE

This is an authentic French recipe from the Oc region.
(Yes, there really is an Oc region. It is known as the Pays
d'Oc and has been making famous and fabulous wine since
the 5th century. It even has its own language – rather like,
and yet unlike, the Welsh – in that you can understand it –
just! However, they share the fact that the spelling is all to
pot.)
But, *"Beer soup!?"* you say. Well, I am just now eating a
pate'-croissant; and that is <u>very</u> Oc.
So, here's how you make Beer Soup for four people: –

-Take one and a half litres of *Gerva d'Oc* ale, along with:
    four egg yolks,
    3 ounces of sugar,
    two 100cl tubs of crème-fraiche,
    a little cinnamon,
    some salt and a bit of pepper.

-Put some of the beer and all the other ingredients into a
saucepan and beat together until smooth.
-Add the remainder of the beer and heat (***but do not boil!***)
until ready to serve.

Serve with a slice of toast – crusty, thick and hearty.
Pour the soup over it – it's what you do!

"Honest to God, it was a delight." [Mary].

-o0o-

Recipe Twenty-eight

WHAT TO DO WITH A LARGE, WILD PUMPKIN

Important note
First of all - for goodness' sake - calm it down a little.

What you must then do

-Saute' 2lb of onions, in bits, in 1/2lb butter* and add 2oz garlic. Try to find some old-style garlic as this modern stuff is so difficult to peel.
-Also add 10oz lardons (little bitz of pork – smoked is best).

*I know they say, *"Please don't cook with Kerrygold."*
But it is jolly good butter and ideal for this dish. So just go ahead and cook with it. What do they know, anyway?

-When the onion is soft, add the following:
    7.5lbs of pumpkin cubes,
    6 pints of water,
    2lbs white beans,
    3tsp of coriander and the same of Ptarragon (from Scotland),
    2tsp of cumin and one of hot chilli powder.
    Grind in some black'n'white pepper and add four vegetable stock cubes.

-Add the five tomatoes that you prepared previously; bring it all to the boil and simmer for a long time.
-If you have any frozen pumpkin pure' from two years ago, now is the time to add that to the mixture.

When it all seems to be done (about two hours later), have some in a bowl and decant the rest into sterilized Kilner-jars and keep until December.
Label it clearly:

Xmas Pumpkin Soup

-or, for purists:

Christmas Pumpkin Soup

Interesting fact

The great thing about this recipe is that, if you forget to use it up, it is available to add to all sorts of other dishes to give them that extra piquancy they sometimes require.

-o0o-

Recipe Twenty-nine

EASY PASTA

What to do

-Boil up some pasta in one pan.
-Fry a chopped onion, along with half a packet of 'lardons' in another pan.
-Add five desert-spoons of tinned chopped-tomatoes to the second pan.
-Drain the pasta from the first pan.
-Mix together in either pan – it really does not matter which.
-Eat it all up.

Now, that really was easy - wasn't it?

The great attribute this dish has over all others is that it never, ever palls.

-o0o-

Recipe Thirty

THE FINEST BUTTERED-EGGS YOU EVER DID TASTE

Description

Although coming from the Mazaudet Country Kitchen, this dish goes back even further. It is the personal recipe of Old Mother Bruen, along with her Tomato Sandwiches and Egg Sandwiches. (Recipe 20)
No-one else has ever been able to reproduce the absolute excellence of this dish to equal OMB. All we can do is try to achieve somewhere near it and to this end the method below is included.

Best of Luck! You should come pretty close and, with practise ... well, who knows?

How you should do it

-Beat up the finest, freshest, country-bred, free-range, corn-fed chickens' eggs with a little cream and some chopped chives.
-Gently - very gently - heat a pan with some butter in the bottom.
-When *'all iss clar'**, pour in the eggs and, still over a low heat, gently 'lift' the cooking egg off the bottom in large flakes – with a spatula.
-Meanwhile, get someone else to make toast and butter it.

-Do not stop 'lifting' but when the mixture has solidified, but **before it becomes dry**, put it onto the toast and dust with black pepper and a very little salt.

Eat immediately.
This will be, absolutely, the finest 'buttered egg' you have ever, ever tasted.
You're welcome.

* *'all iss clar'* - This is a technical term that refers to the state of melted butter before it starts to 'brown'.

-o0o-

Recipe Thirty-one

Mrs BRUEN'S CELEBRATED FUDGE PUDDING

Description

Once again, this is one of the finest recipes on the planet; which is not surprising when you consider it comes from OMB via the Mazaudet Country Kitchen. Further, it must rank with *Glenfarg Pudding* as one of the simplest to make.

Therefore, with that in mind and considering that you must have picked up an enormous amount of know-how having read thus far, *Fudge Pudding* will be presented in its briefest form – easy to remember, see?

Historical note

In days gone by, when ever guests arrived at the Chateau Bruen (in deepest Worcestershire) for a Dinner Party, the first question they always asked on stepping over the threshold was, *"Are we having 'Fudge Pudding' tonight?"*

Now, if you can engender that sort of enthusiasm for this dish, then you are a worthy successor to Mother Bruen as a presenter of the finest dessert available anywhere, anytime - ever.

This is how you do it

-Make a pint of un-seasoned 'white sauce', by hand – not from a packet.

-Heat the contents of a 1lb tin of Lyles Golden Syrup in another pan until it boils; then add it to the white sauce, stirring it in well.

-Gently cook this until it is coffee-coloured and then add a good squeeze of 'Jiffy' lemon-juice – **perhaps the most important ingredient of all!**

-Turn into a decorated bowl and allow to cool and to set.

-Once cold, smother with a thick layer of grated Bourneville chocolate.

Serve with large amounts of real, sugarless whipped cream and hear your guests' exclamations of sheer delight. Well done!

And Finally Recipe Thirty-two

NOTTALOTT-STEW

Description

Here is another gem from the *'Let's-eat-right-away'* School of Cookery, as practised by the Mazaudet International Cross-country Cooking Fraternity. This recipe is so simple that it is ridiculous. The only difficult part is to remember to soak the Peas and Beans overnight. If you forget to do this, do not worry. They will still be quite edible but just a little crunchier than usual.

What you will need

Collect together the following:
A quarter of a pint of Lentils. (Good-old Lentils, eh?)
Two dozen dried, split Yellow Peas
Three dried Broad Beans
One and a half handfuls of mixed Macaroni and Spaghetti bits (anything that's left over, really)
A tiny tin of Tomato Paste
Half a teaspoon of Onion Salt
A teaspoon of Pepper
A teaspoon of Salt
Two shakes of Basil
Three shakes of Marjoram
One and a half pints of Water

One and a half large pinches of Chilli-powder
A glug of Olive Oil
Hot Worcestershire Sauce

Now that you have arranged for all the above to be in the same place at the same time, no doubt you are wondering:-

What next?

-Empty the whole lot into a saucepan in the usual MCK fashion and put it onto a high heat until it starts to bubble.
-Now turn it down to about half-heat (or slide a trivet under it), so that it does not boil-over and make a mess of your galley, and give it an occasional stir.
-When the spaghetti is soft you can take it off and eat it; otherwise let it cook for a little longer and to thicken-up a bit.

Useful tip. You may like to add more salt or pepper to season the brew; not to worry - just go ahead and do whatever you like to it. You will certainly enjoy this simple and nourishing meal and will not find it boring for repetition; and it's so e-e-e-easy!

Note: if it does, by chance, become boring, add the good old Curry Powder to it; problem solved.

-o0o-

Final note:

If you have found that these recipes are rather 'samey', don't worry. You are probably right but it does not make them any the less delicious. It is, after all, Mazaudet Cross-country Cuisine Cooking at its best and there is nowhere else in the world that produces anything like it. There ain't many Chefs who can say that.

THE LAST RESORT

So there we have the Expat, well prepared for anything that might be thrown at him, at peace with himself and firmly in control of the situation. It has taken time but he is there at last.

During his Travels, he will have come across places that he dislikes, some places that he positively hates but a good many that are really 'jolly good!' (as Doctor Chris would have it). He will have written in his Memory Book some descriptive pieces, factual accounts of his Adventures and a number of 'aide memoire' to let him do just that. It is also possible that he may have been so effected by certain situations that he branched out into verse, in an effort to capture the essence of the moment.

Here, as an example, is such a Poem, instigated by the acceptance of our Traveller into the Morai of a New Zealand tribe by their Headwoman, who went by the evocative name of – *'Kuinie'* – and gave him the Moari name of – *'Heremana'* – the 'Brave Sailor'.

IN SEARCH OF THE MAORI

Where is the bird whose unfinished whistle
Calls to the people born of the woodland,

Asking the question, time past repeating,
'Where have you fled, better to rest?'

See the bright songster high in the tree-top,
Trilling his chanson, phrase without meaning;
Not his the question nor his the caring.
Unseen the bird, endless the quest.

Empty the answer under the branches
From the lost people, gone from the forest;
Only an echo'd note on the evening,
'Come to us. Fly southerly–west.'

But wherever he may have been, whatever Tropical Paradise he may have visited, with whichever Country he may have fallen in love, there still remains that ever elusive Haven which tugs firmly and incessantly at his sleeve and calls to him in the waking hour, long before dawn, as the 'punkah-fan' squeaks maddeningly overhead and the chit-chats chirrup,
"Home, home, home......" It is the place to which his thoughts turn again and forever, and nothing else can ever match up to its singular allure.
For our Traveller it was ....

A SAILOR'S DREAM OF DEVON

To Plymouth I was bound, one clear and frosty day.
I loaded fiddle, 'bag and tent and soon was on my way.
The miles passed one by one; they mounted score on score
And as they vanished in the dusk, I thought the more and
more
Of Devon far away.

And when I reached the end of that half-a-thousand miles,
My pulse a-race, my eyes a-shine, my face awash with
smiles,
The happy hours passed quickly, and the memory will
remain,
But every parting broke my heart and made me long again
For Devon far away.

We'd sailed the rippling Sound and walked the Dartmoor
hills.
We'd camped beneath the winter sky when all the world
was still'd;
But every jar of ale and every Pub we knew
Engraved the letters on my heart, for now I know it's true;
That Devon's far away.

And now, though half the world between us surely lies,
A day is never passing but my mind to Devon flies.
If I perchance am home-sick, caught a-luff, be-calmed, in
stays,

Then let me languish under that strange illness all my days, -
If Devon's far away.

O Devon, far away, the land where I would go;
The places where the music will enliven every heart;
Where the friendship of a few means more that they will know;
Where journeys have their ending, but where all of mine must start.

-o0o-

Ectopic – an anomaly of situation
Ectopia --- a nice place to be

-oOo-

We set a sail and see where it takes us.
We make friends and then we move on.
All we can do is remember as best we can.

BB.

This has been a
Solomon Grundy Inc.
Production

enabled by
Dream Circus Posters
Pershore Road
Birmingham

'Dream the Dream; for it will never dream
of you.'

Printed in Great Britain
by Amazon

79428096R00190